# Early 5-String Banjo Solos

## In Historic 19th Century Stroke, Clawhammer and Guitar Styles

by

Tim Twiss

**To access the online audio recording go to:**
***WWW.MELBAY.COM/30991MEB***

*WWW.MELBAY.COM*

# INTRODUCTION

This work came about from studying the written record of 19th Century Banjo music. In particular, I mention the Briggs' book of 1855, Rice 1858, the Buckley books of 1860 and 1868, and the Converse books of 1865. There is also the understated *Banjoist's Budget* by A. Baur of 1883 and most importantly, the Converse *Analytical Method* of 1886.

Conceptually, I learned everything I know about the banjo from these books, where instructions were presented in great detail, providing precious insight into 19th century banjo playing. This book is the manifestation of that study. Please keep an open mind and allow this music to become an ongoing vibrant and living tradition.

- **The Music**: The content of this book was chosen from music available c. 1840 – 1890. I used multiple sources, as shown in the index. The variety of pieces chosen was the result of seeking and uncovering material comparable to what was in the original tutors or method books. When I refer to "other sources" in the index, I mean original versions found in the Lester Levy Collection as well as the digital libraries around the country that have catalogued and made them available. It should be mentioned that I also use "field observations" of people playing this music today, as well as the available historic recordings.
- **Style**: This book includes simple songs meant to be sung, which were made popular by sheet music sales and performances on the minstrel stage. The simpler vocal tunes such as "Long Tail Blue" and "Southern Rose" are arranged very much in the style of Briggs, allowing the melody to be the dominant feature supplemented by rhythmic figures utilizing the thumb string. They also function as an accompaniment to singing. Some tunes are directly taken from European sources such as jigs, reels, and hornpipes. As Buckley and Converse did, I include Schottisches, polkas, and strathspeys. I've also included some arrangements from the light classics that stretch the possibilities of the instrument.
- **Choice of Material:** Each piece was chosen for its unique effect upon the listener and the joy of execution on the banjo. I did not want to end up with 50 banjo songs that sound the same. Colorful and memorable melodies must "lie well" on the instrument. When selecting them, it was necessary to have a good "fit" to the instrument without compromising the content. Forcing an arrangement to fit these parameters was unacceptable. Playability is of utmost importance.
- **Originals:** It was common practice for authors to include their own music. I followed suit and placed two of mine in the mix. They are written in a style congruent to the rest of the book.
- **Interpretation:** I believe that once the notes land on the banjo, they should leave with a new voice. The banjo has a sound quality unique unto itself. It is melody *and* rhythm expressed in perfect union. Great speed and long sustained notes are not naturally strong points for this instrument. Rather than force it to be something other than what it is, let us celebrate the peculiar voice that it has. Some of the fiddle tunes intended to be played fast turn out to have a beautiful quality when played slowly, much like looking at something under a microscope. You will see and hear things that are not made apparent when playing at a blistering tempo. The counterpoint and integrity of the piece, however, must be strong. This may be both right *and* wrong, but I hope the player will find freedom and beauty in the abandonment of common interpretation. Let the instrument growl and sing joyfully with imperfections. The only restriction I place upon the player, is to honor the articulations and use reasonable musical discretion.

- **Technique:** One should be competent in basic **stroke** and **guitar style** of play. There is great debate about the practice and application of these techniques, and rather than corner the player into a dogmatic approach, the choice remains open. Some are obvious, others not so much. There is a GREAT JOY in discovery, and I do not want to deprive the player of that experience. On many pieces, I play the *hybrid* style, meaning I switch from stroke to guitar style within the same arrangement.
- **Notation and Fingerings**: One will notice the lack of fingerings and markings. This is intentional. Many players disregard them anyway. In my opinion, they can clutter the page unnecessarily. String and position markings are needed in notation, but that information is intrinsic with TAB. Utilizing slurs, hammer-ons, and pull-offs will bring magic and life to the music. I completely work out the articulations I consider essential.
- **Arrangements:** DO NOT FEAR THE LEAPS AND JUMPS. Celebrate them. Know that they have been worked out in advance and, with a reasonable amount of practice, can be smoothly executed. Enjoy the physicality of the instrument. It should be as fun to watch as it is to play.
- **The Instrument**: The banjo used to make the recordings for this book is a custom-made instrument of my own conception; it was built by Terry Bell and Jeff Branch, two talented Michigan luthiers who never actually met. Essentially, it is a fretted minstrel banjo embodying the characteristics of an instrument that evolved in the mid-19th Century.

  I asked for a 25.5" scale length and a 13" rim as opposed to the 26.375" scale and 11" rim found on modern banjos. The instrument was made with fewer brackets or hooks than a modern banjo, and has an open back, friction pegs and a natural skin head. While the details were entirely of their own design, Terry made the rim and roughed out the neck and sent it to Jeff, who did the neck, fret, and inlay work. Jeff then sent the nearly completed instrument back to Terry, who assembled and finished it. The unique element of this otherwise "early" instrument is the addition of 22 frets.

  Early minstrel banjos were completely fretless. The exact date of the appearance of frets on the banjo is not known for certain, but innovation was almost a daily event in those rapidly changing times. Simple music like that found in the *Briggs Banjo Instructor* of 1855 grew into more complex material and the range was extended beyond the 5th fret. I needed frets to play with greater precision and less stress in the upper register.

  Terry and Jeff perfectly addressed my needs with an instrument that reaches for higher ground, just as the music itself evolved away from being played in the lower positions only. My Bell-Branch minstrel banjo growls with a deeper sound, using gut or Nylgut strings authentically tuned to eAEG♯B, the tuning indicated by almost all of the early banjo tutors. The instrument also responds well when tuned higher to gCGBD, the modern C tuning with the 4th string a step lower than the typical G tuning. Except for "Durang's Hornpipe," I used the C tuning to make the companion recording for this book.
- **Form**: I encourage freedom within the prescribed form you see presented. Many of these are of a simple binary arrangement, typically AABB and repeated as needed. I do not always include repeat signs. Even when I do, the performance may drift from that. I often prefer the form of AABABB, but might change it on a whim.

Timothy Twiss / January 2021

The publisher presents this music because of its historical significance in the field of banjo literature. Some titles, although historic and related to this period, have been altered due to their offensive nature.

# Table of Contents



**Bold titles are the easiest to play.**

# Angelina Baker

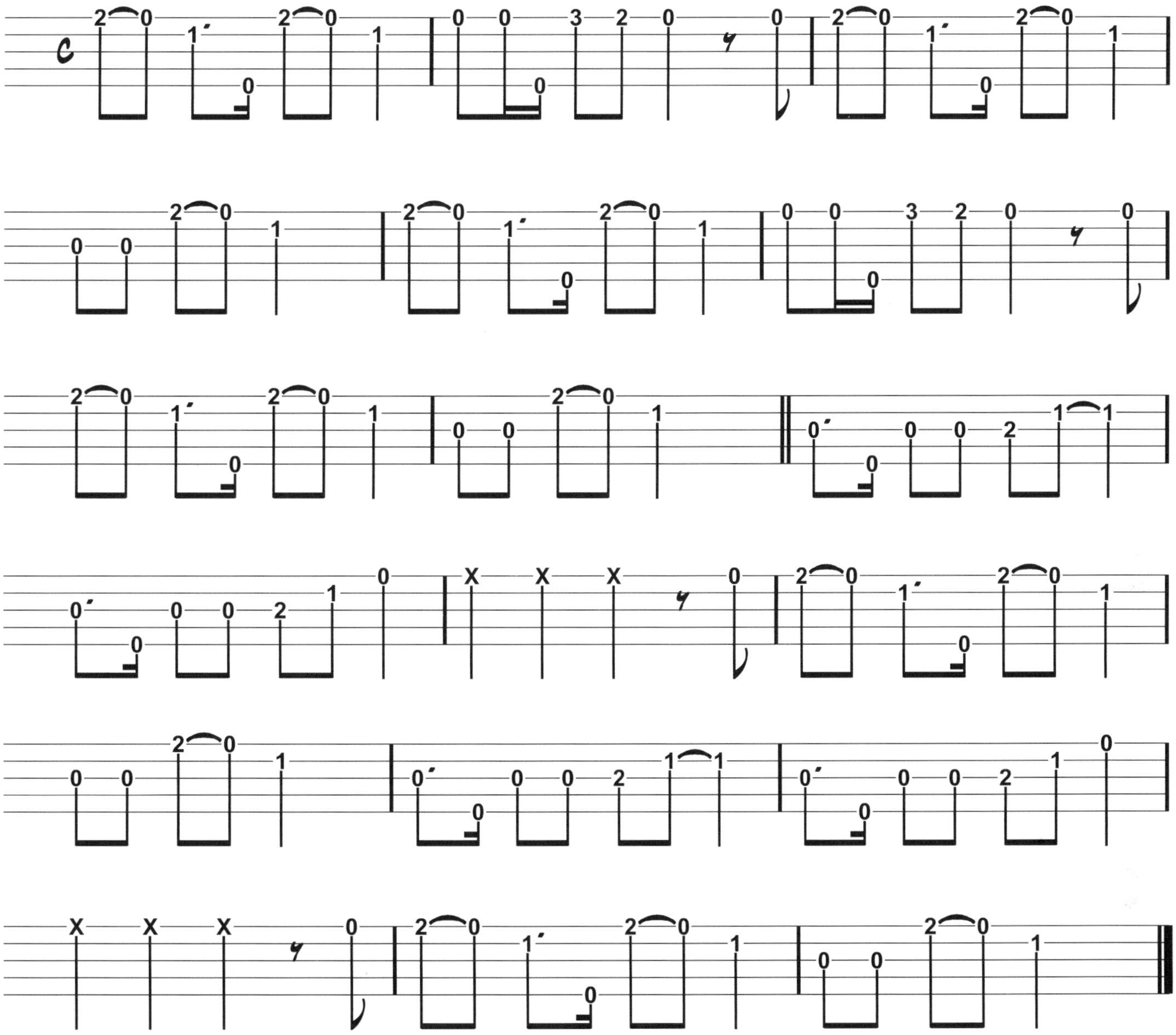

# Back Side of Albany

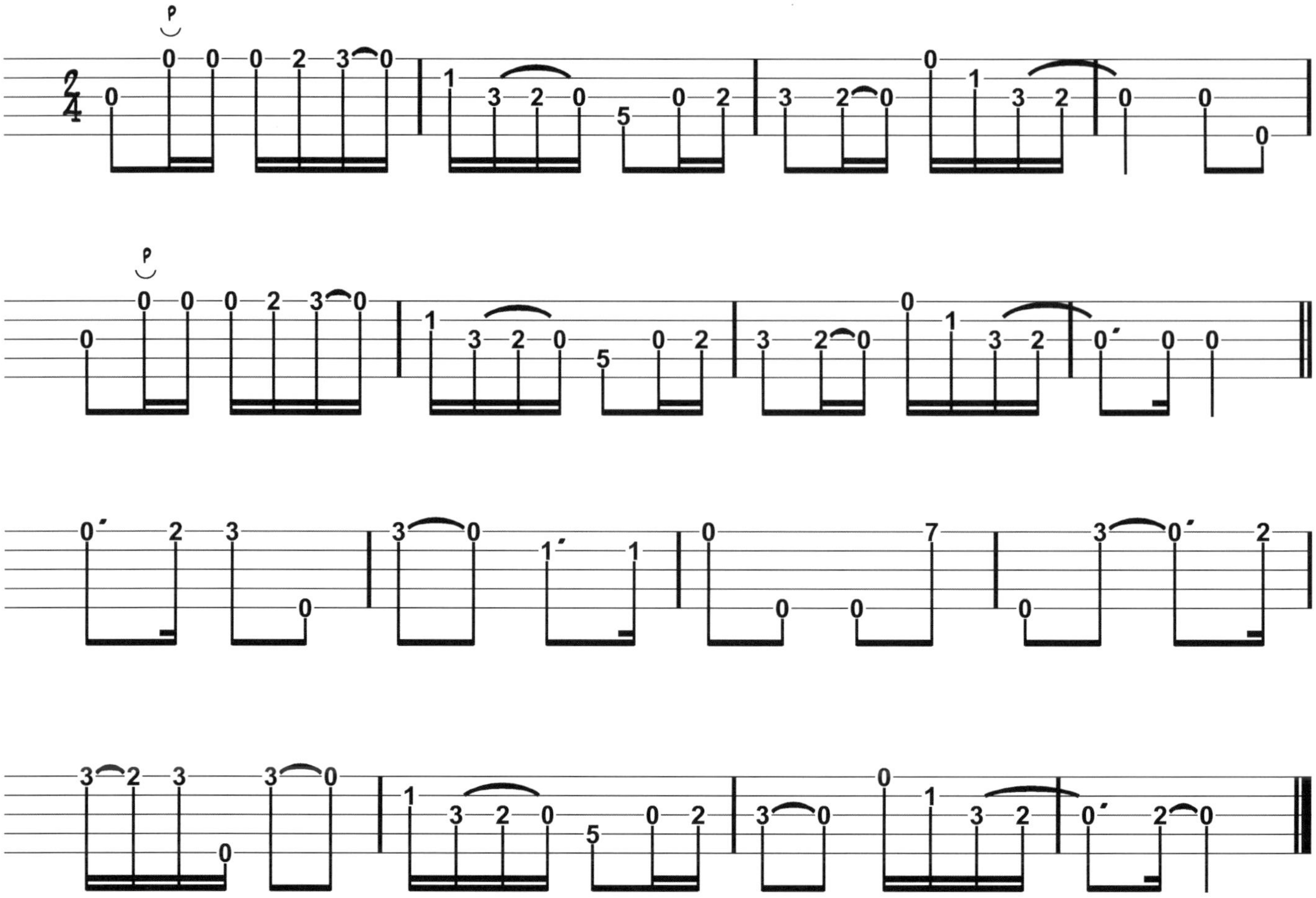

# Battle Cry of Freedom

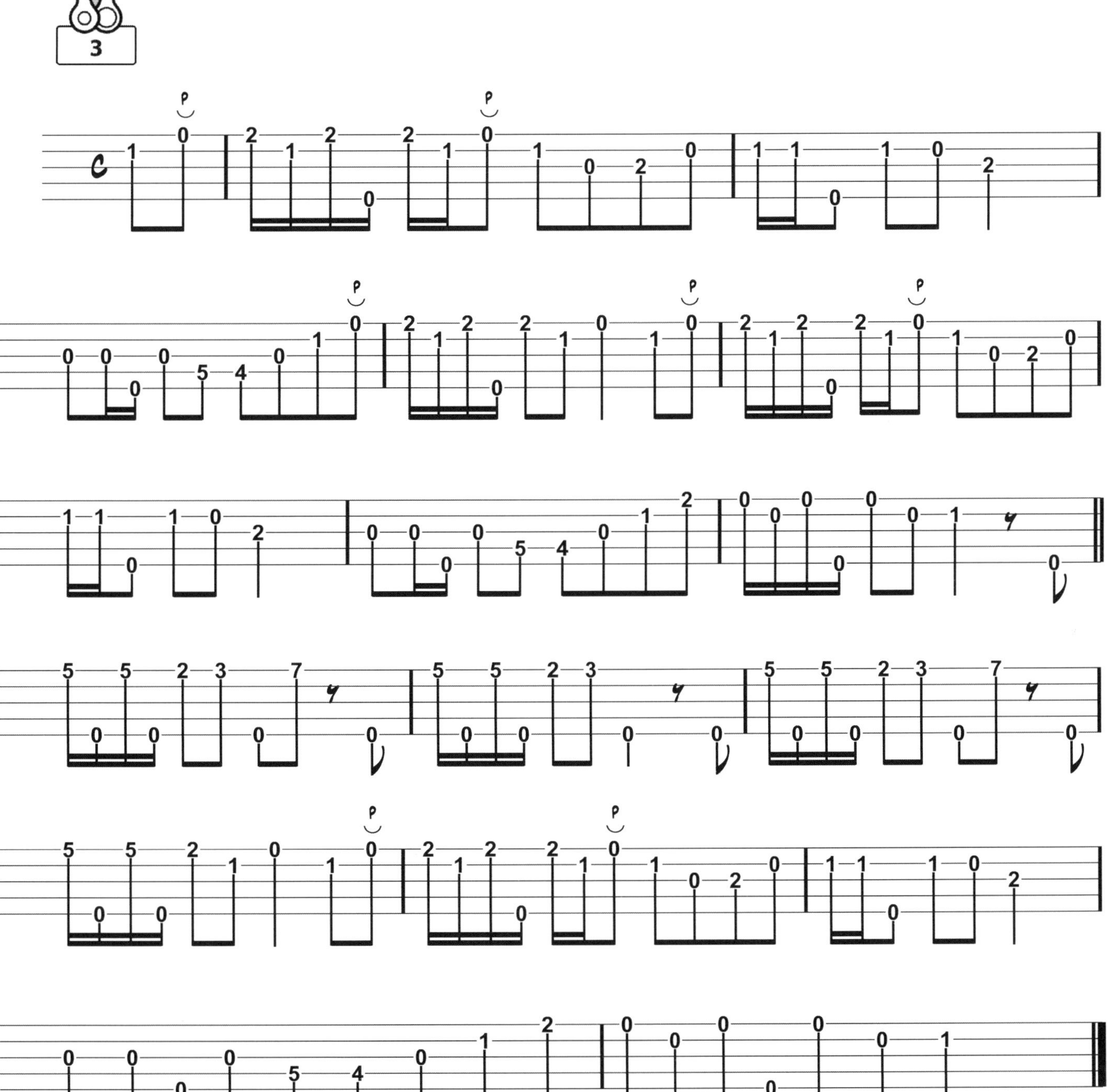

# BATTLE HYMN OF THE REBUBLIC

4

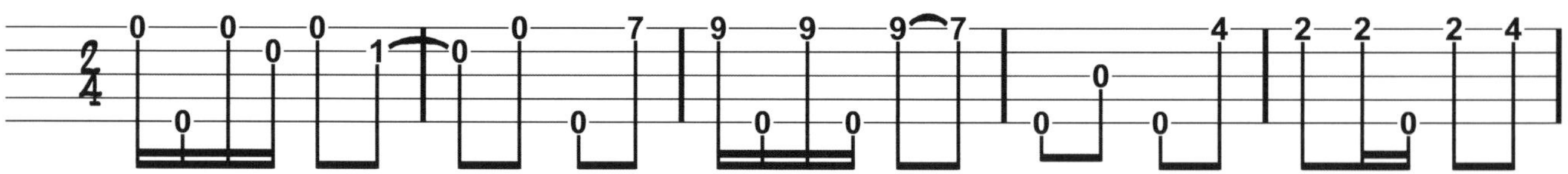

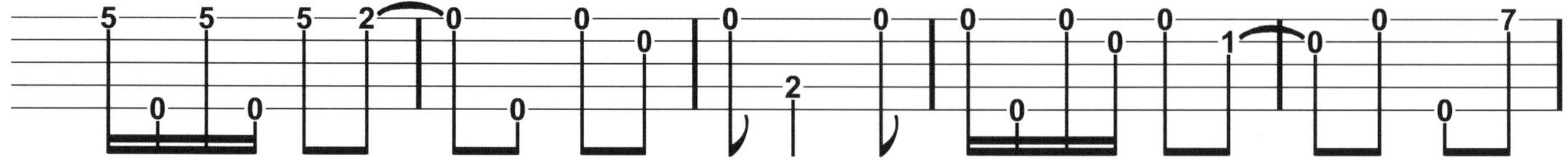

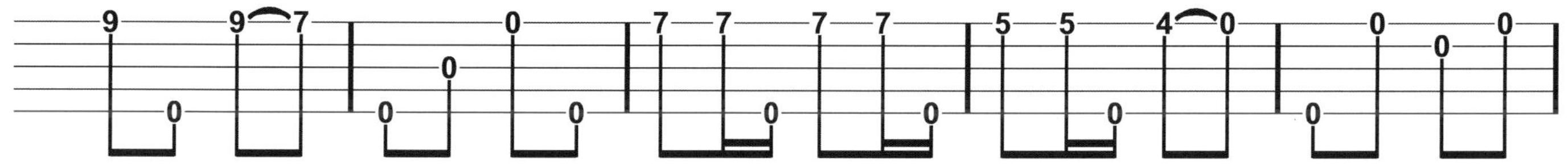

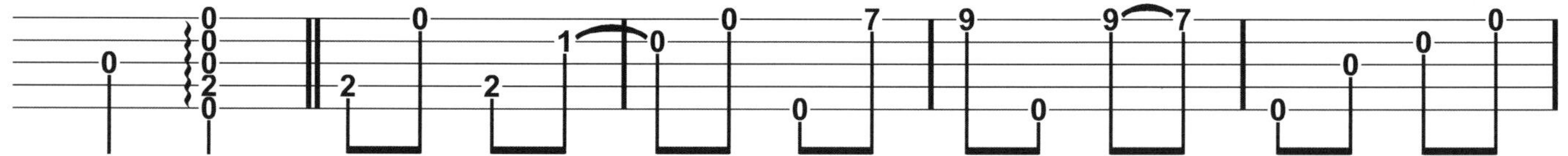

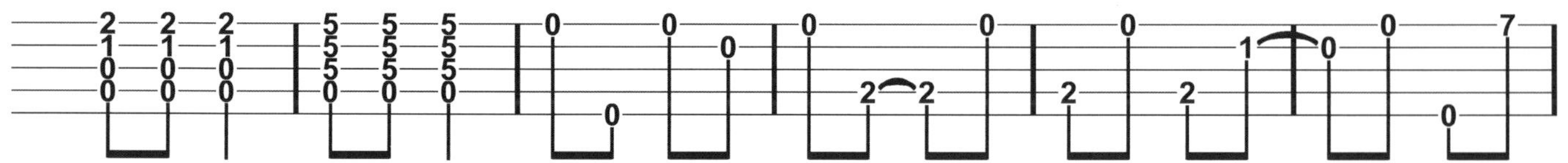

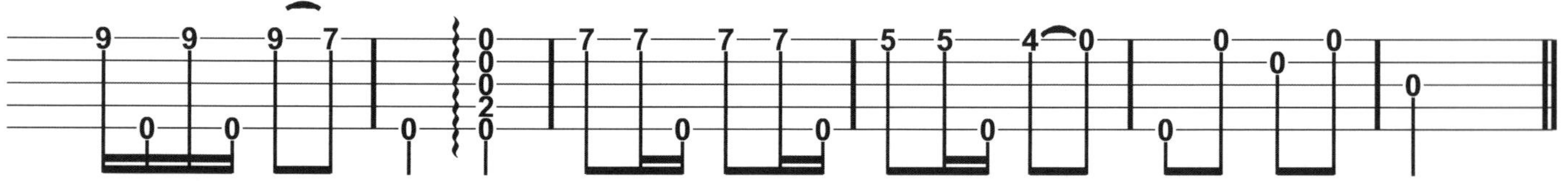

# Bird on the Wing Jig

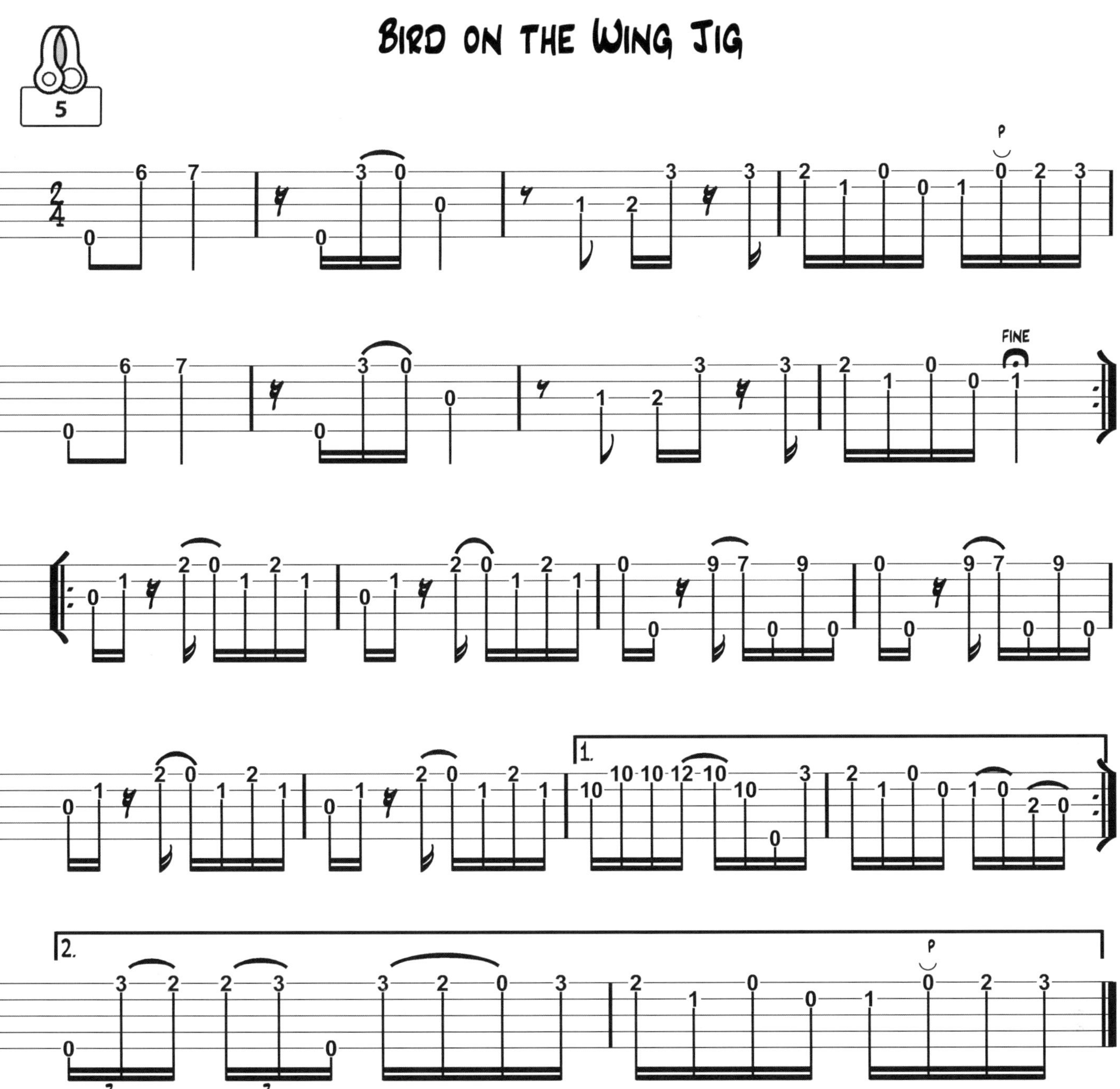

# Bob Chadduck's Jig

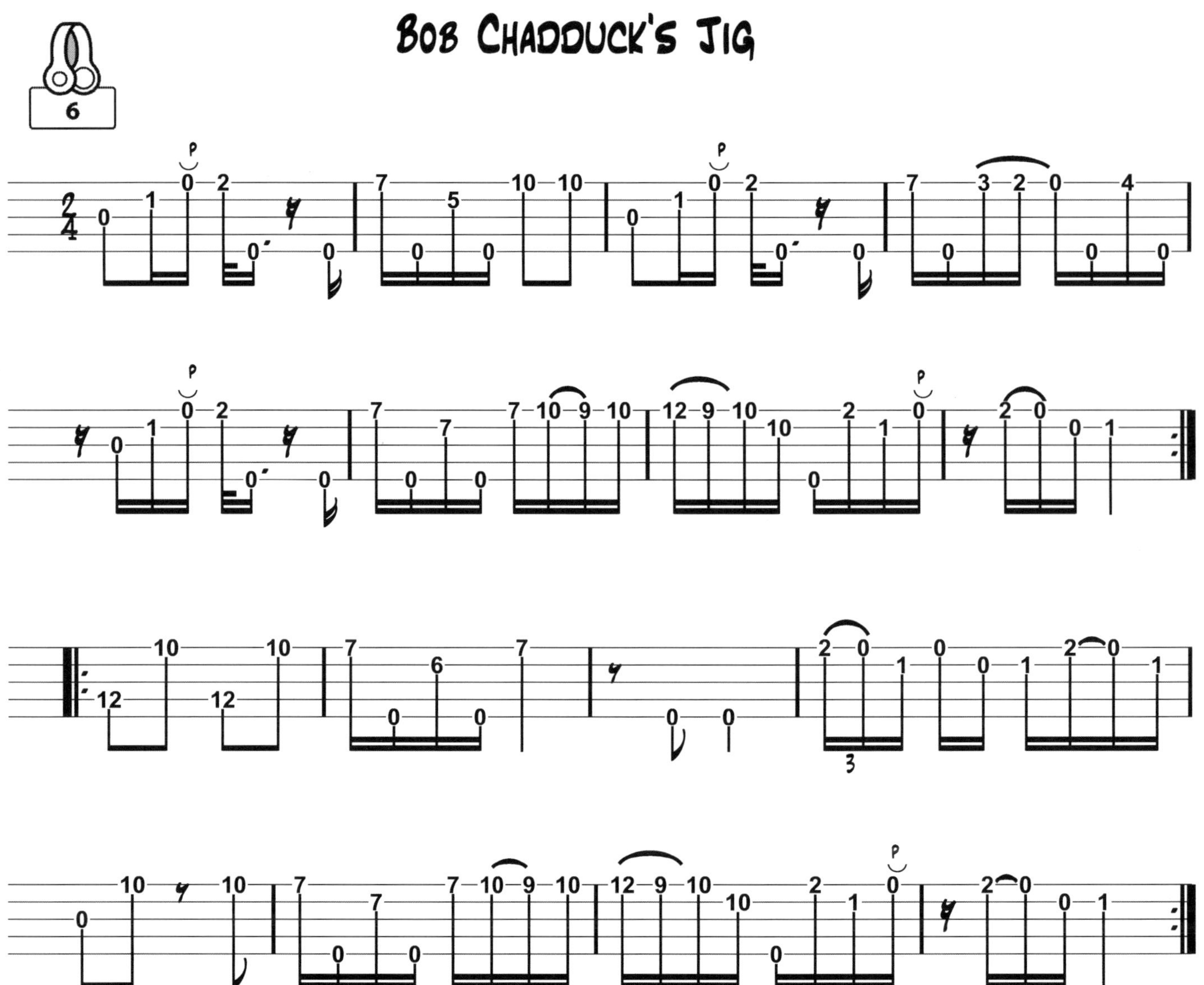

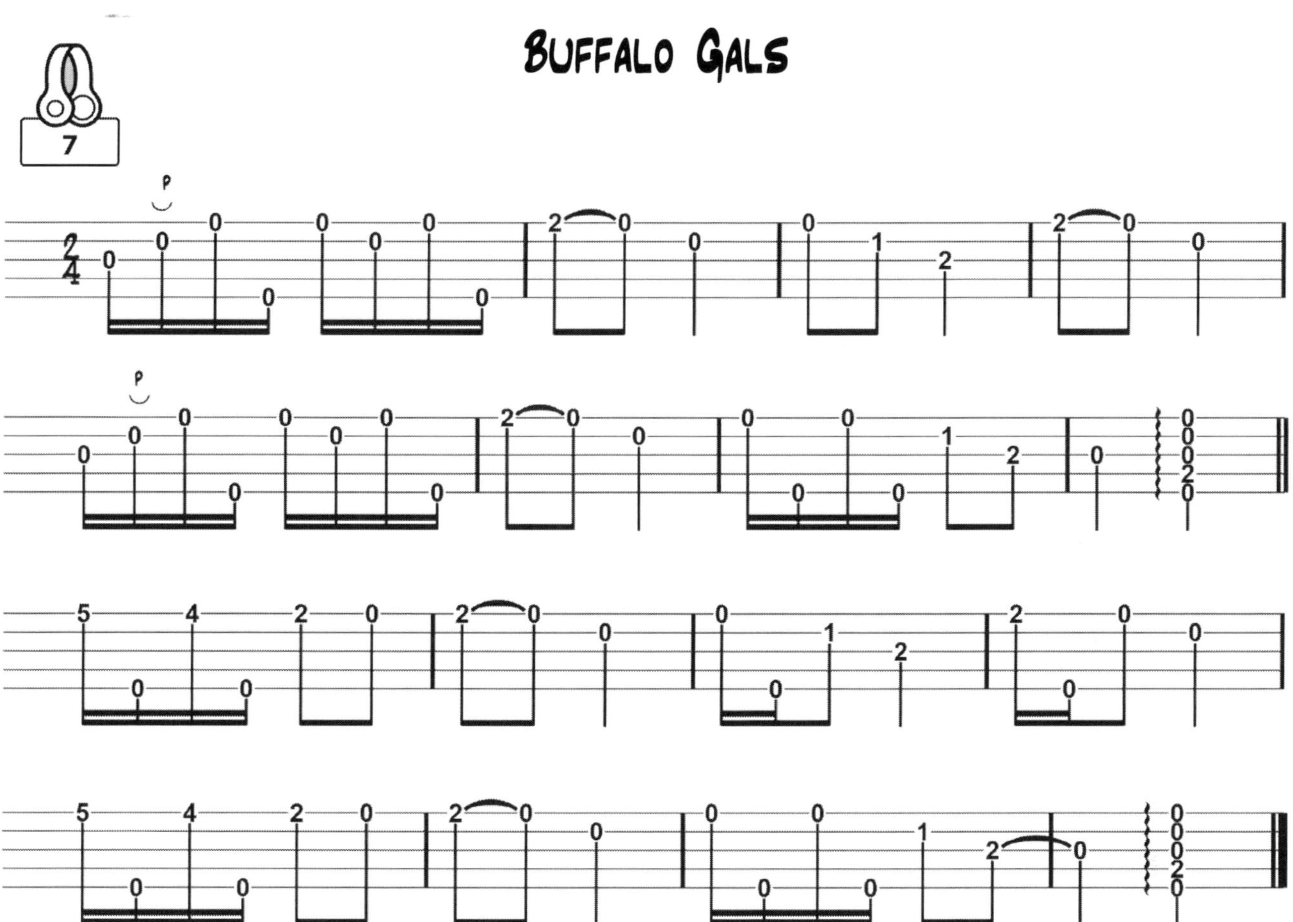
Buffalo Gals
7

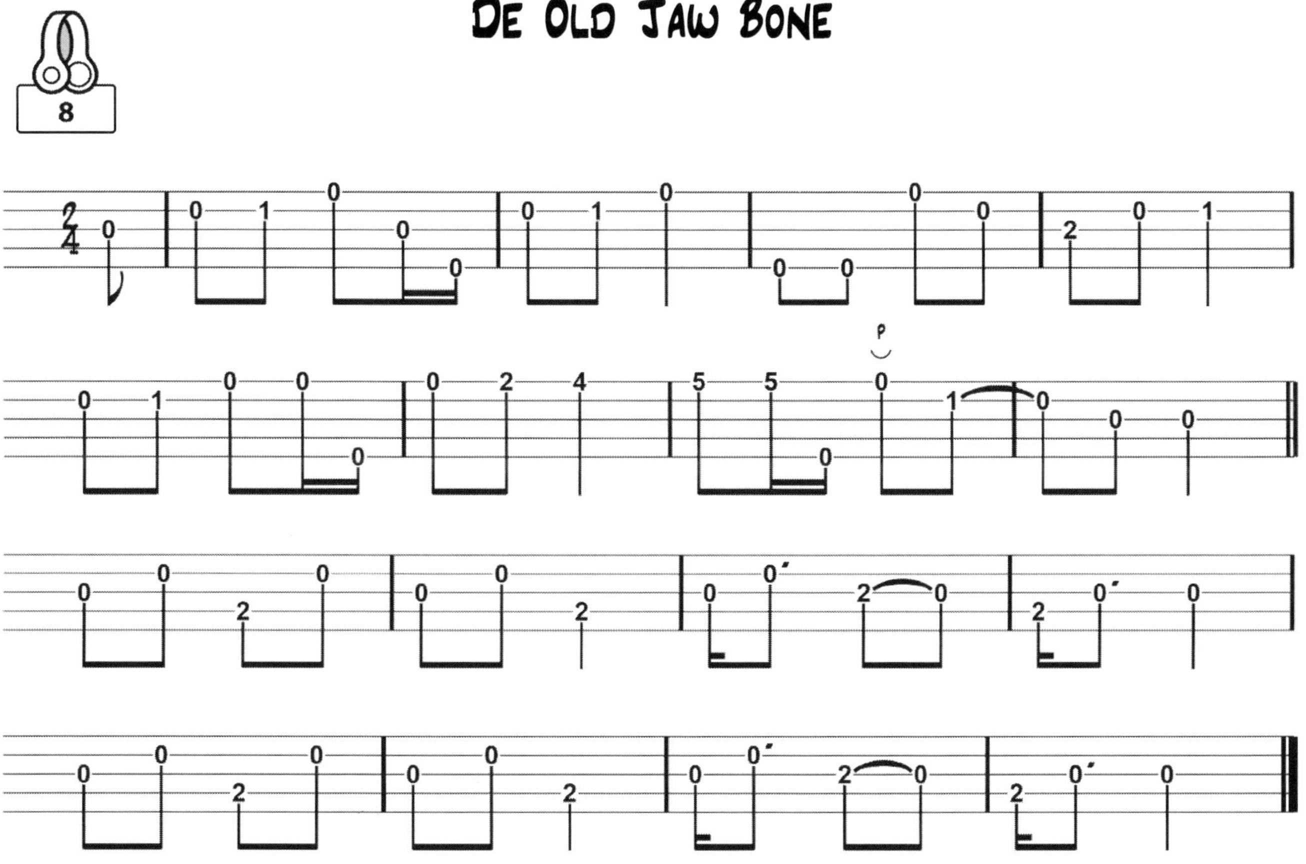
De Old Jaw Bone
8

# Captain Francis Wemyss

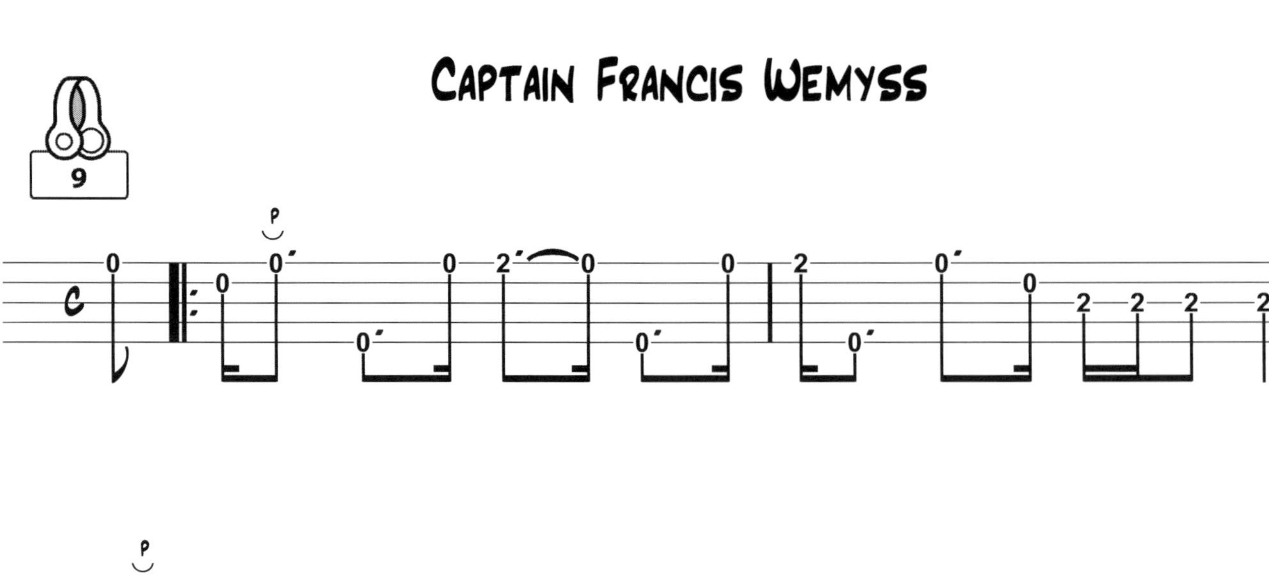


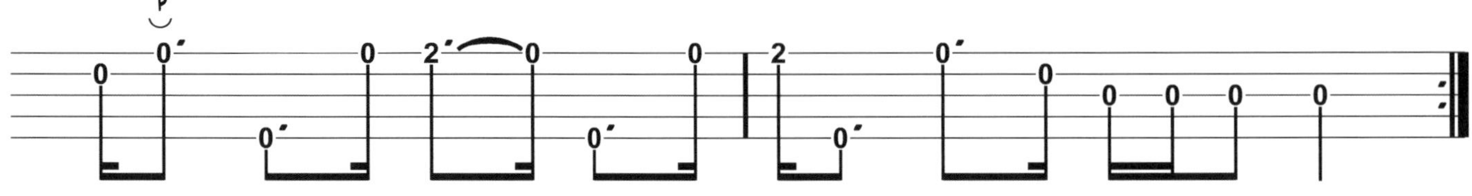

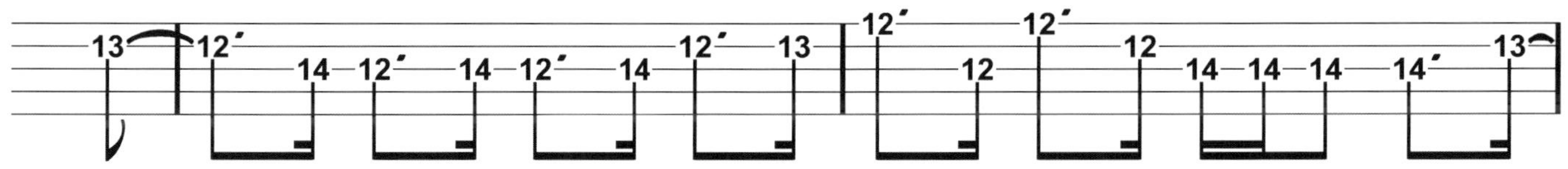

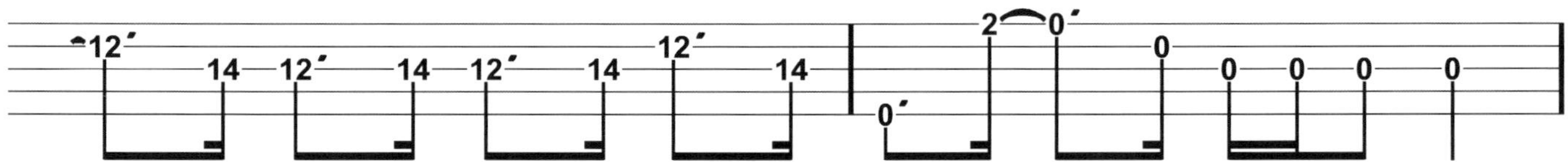

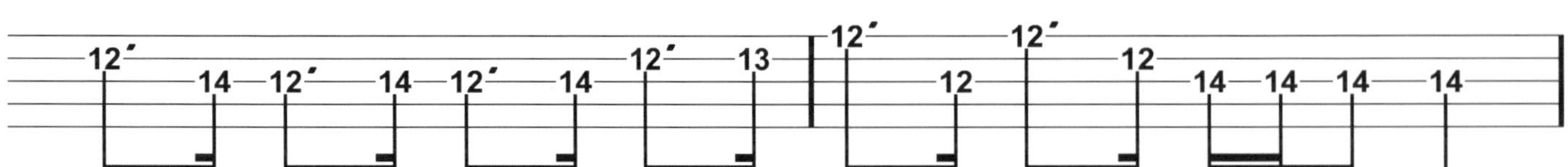

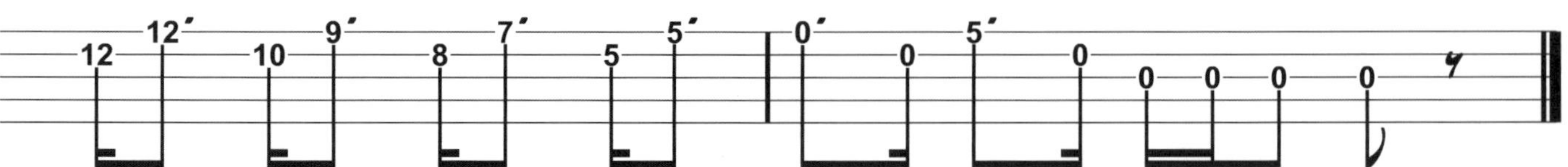

# Castles in the Air

10

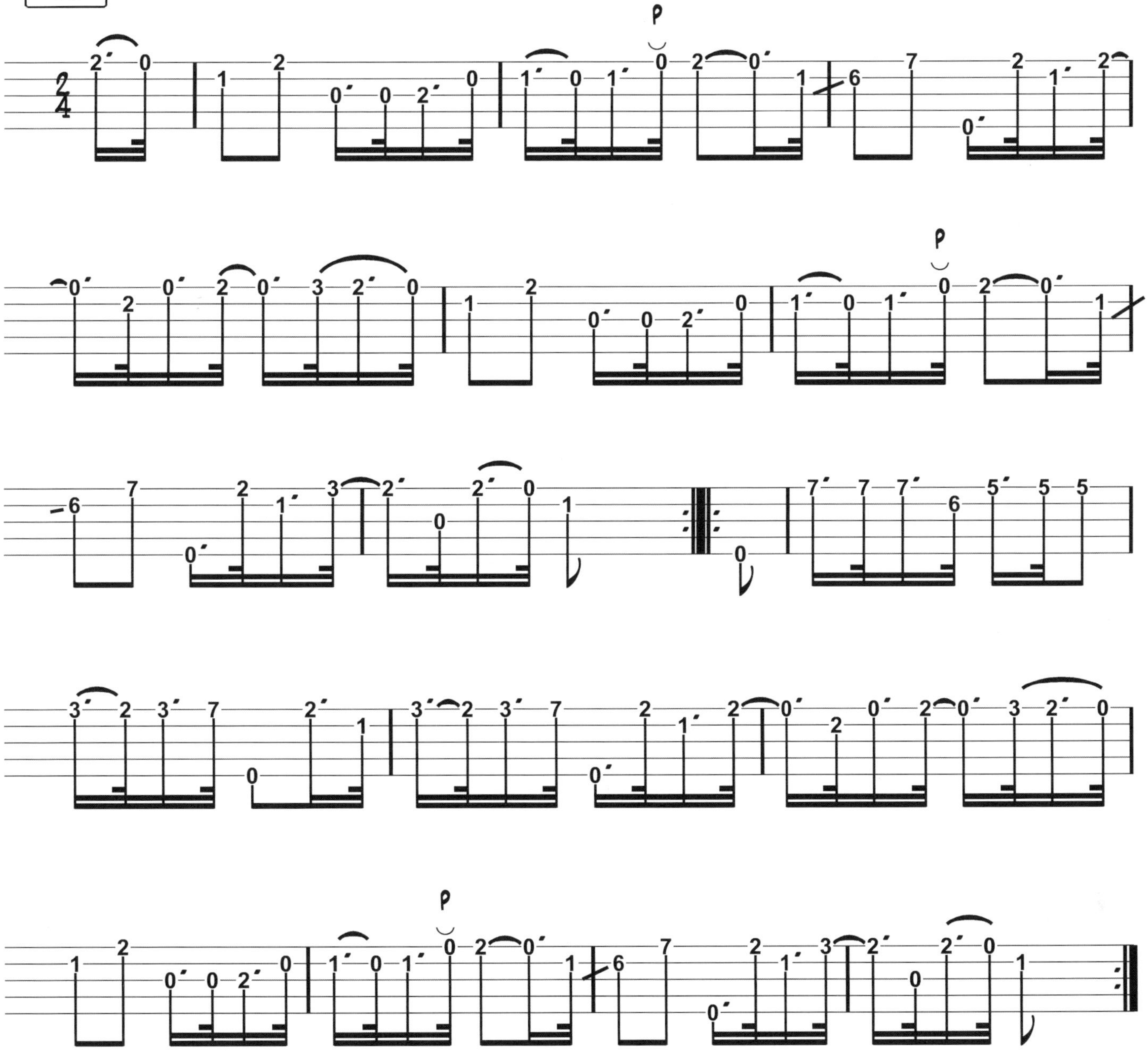

# Copper's Minor

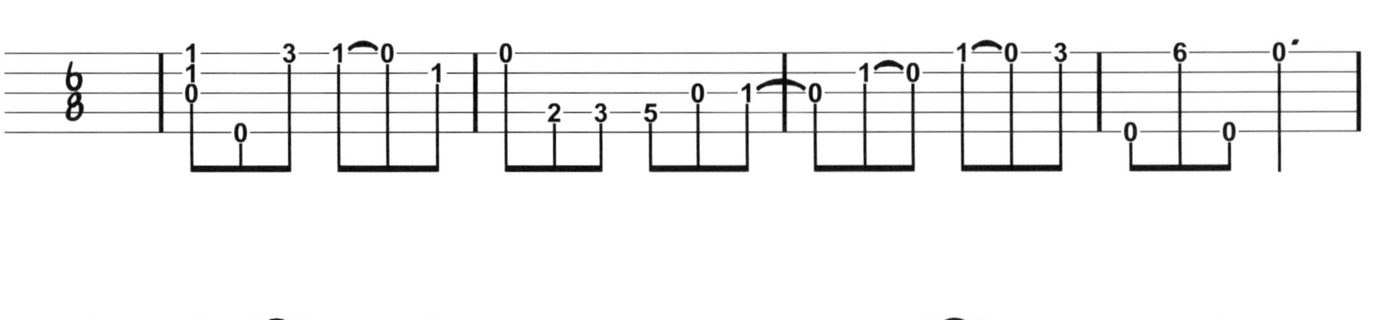

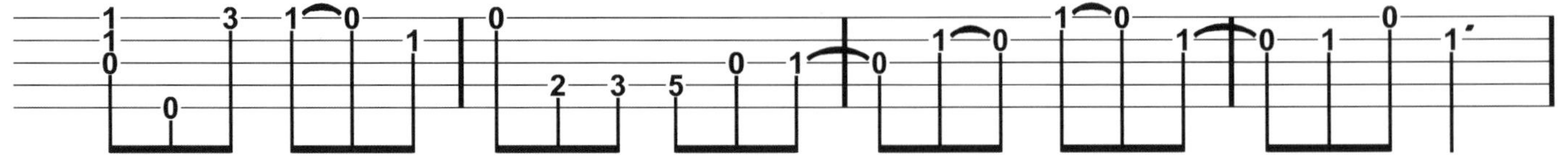

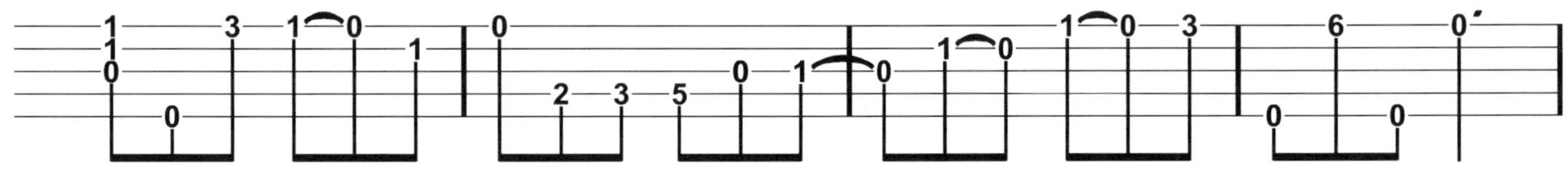

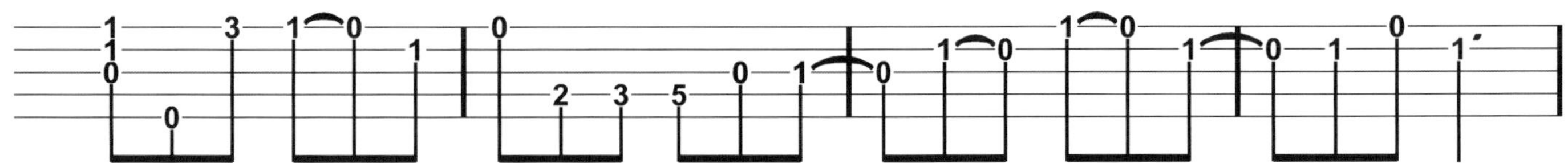

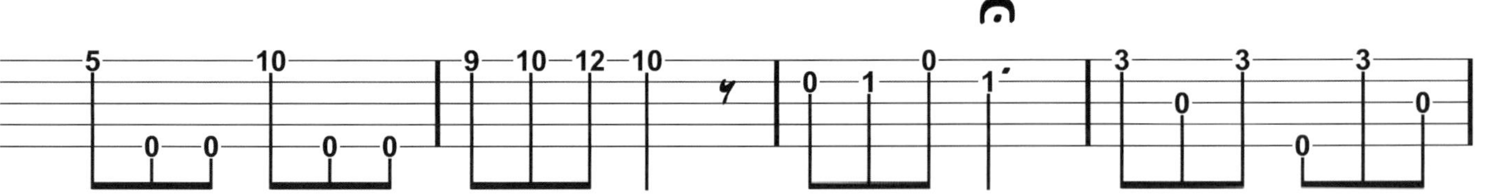

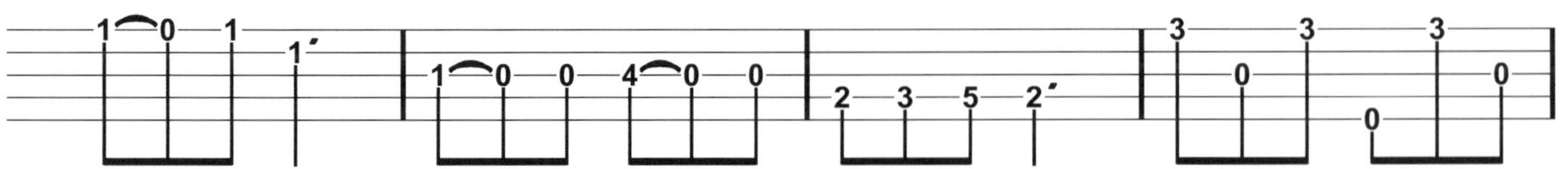

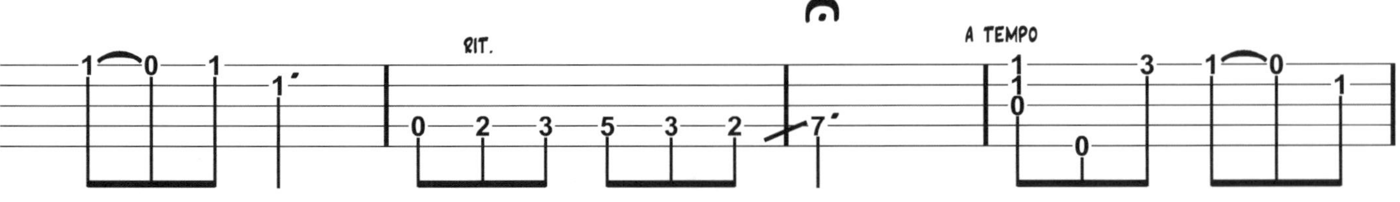

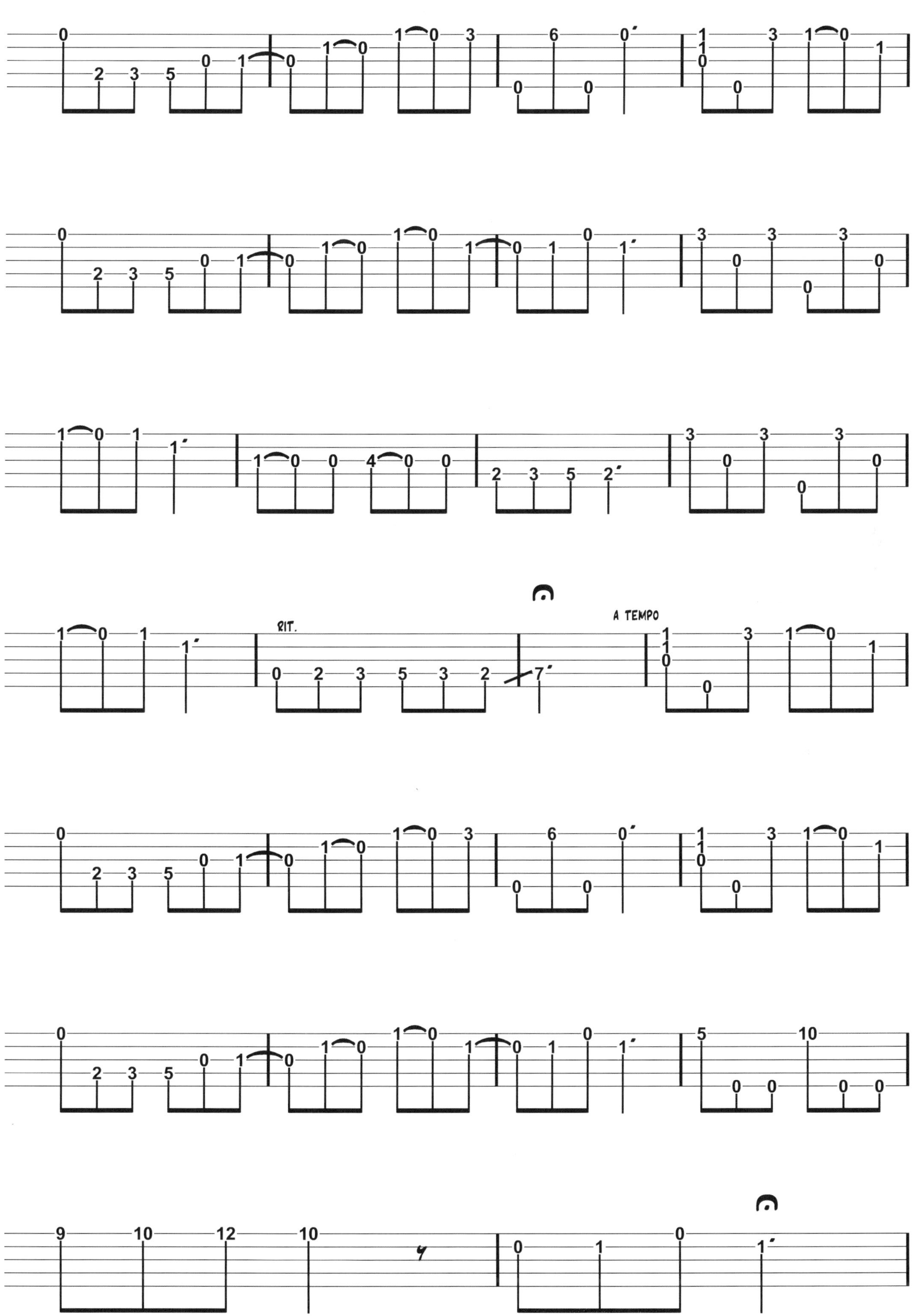
RIT.
A TEMPO

# CRACOVIENNE QUICKSTEP

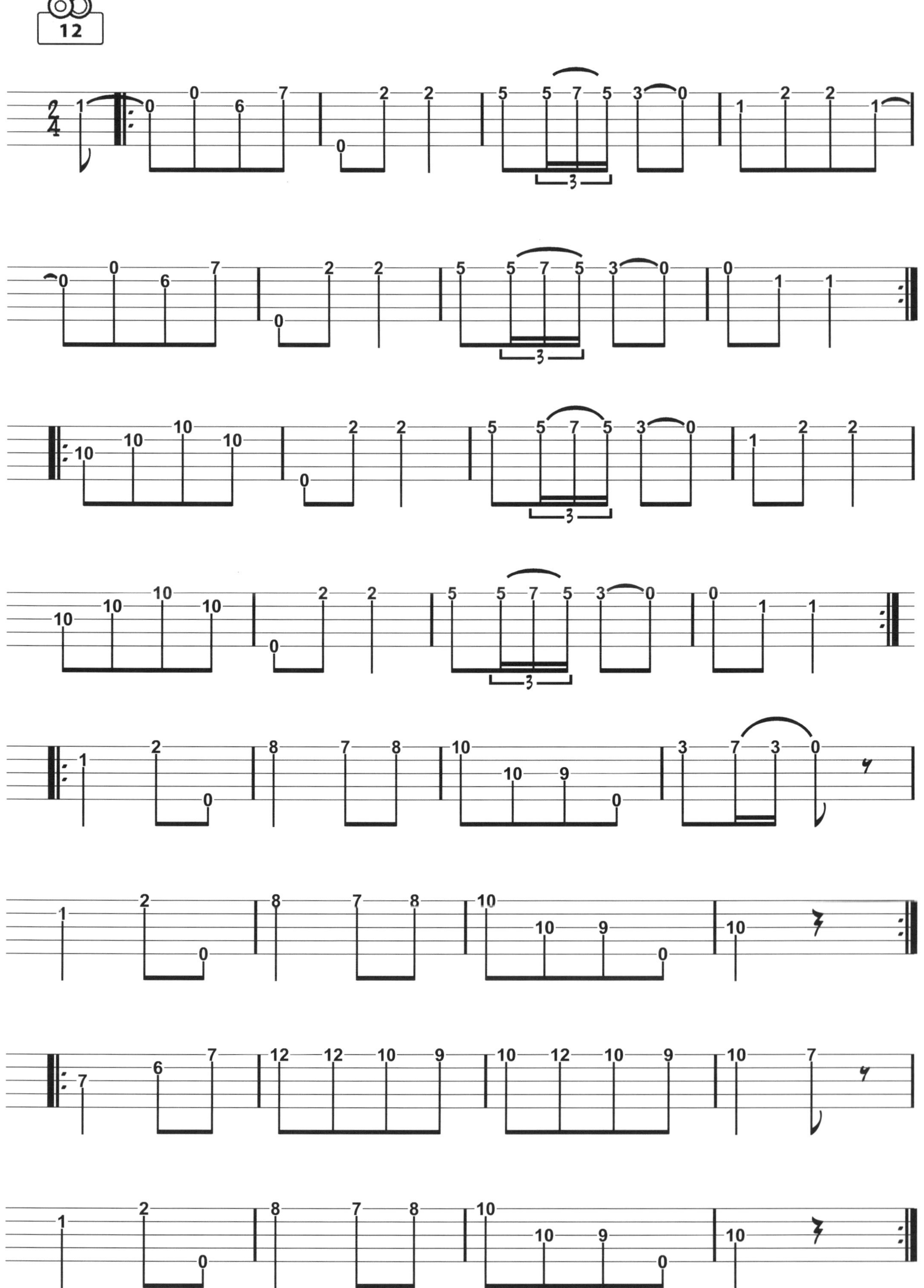

13

# Durang's Hornpipe

High Bass (tune 4th string up one whole step)

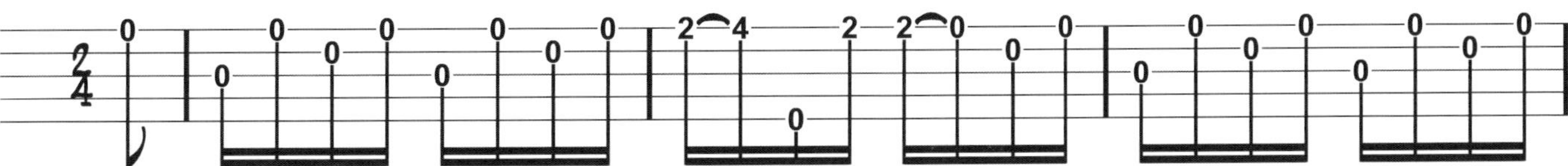

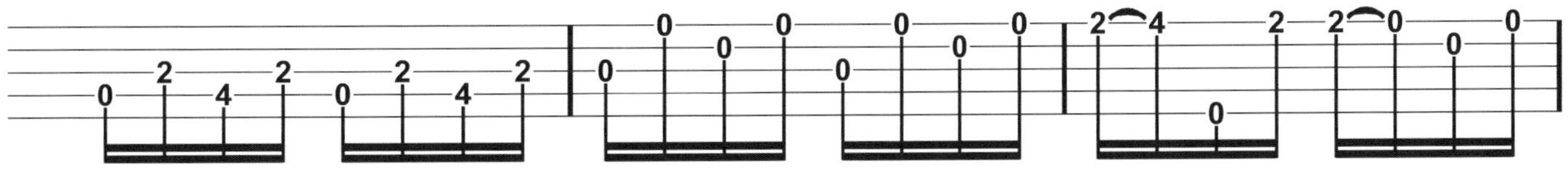

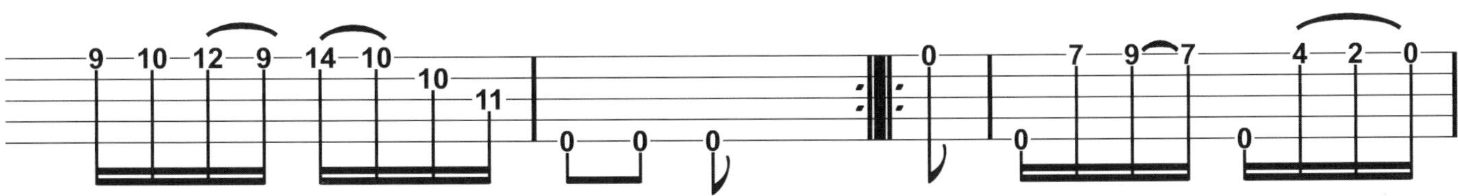

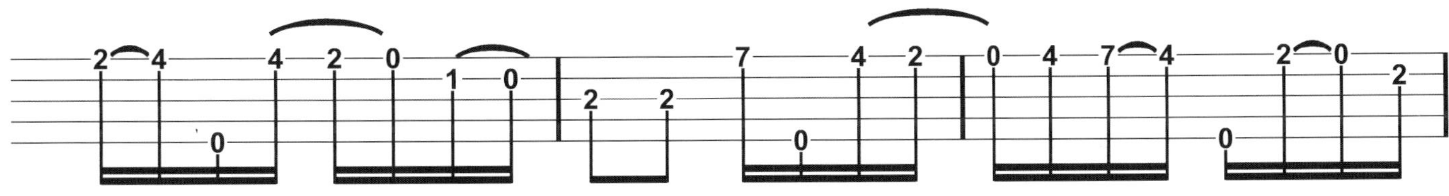

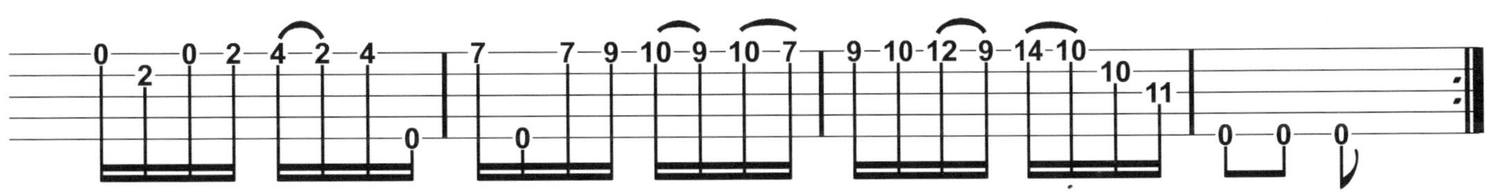

# Essence of Old Kentucky

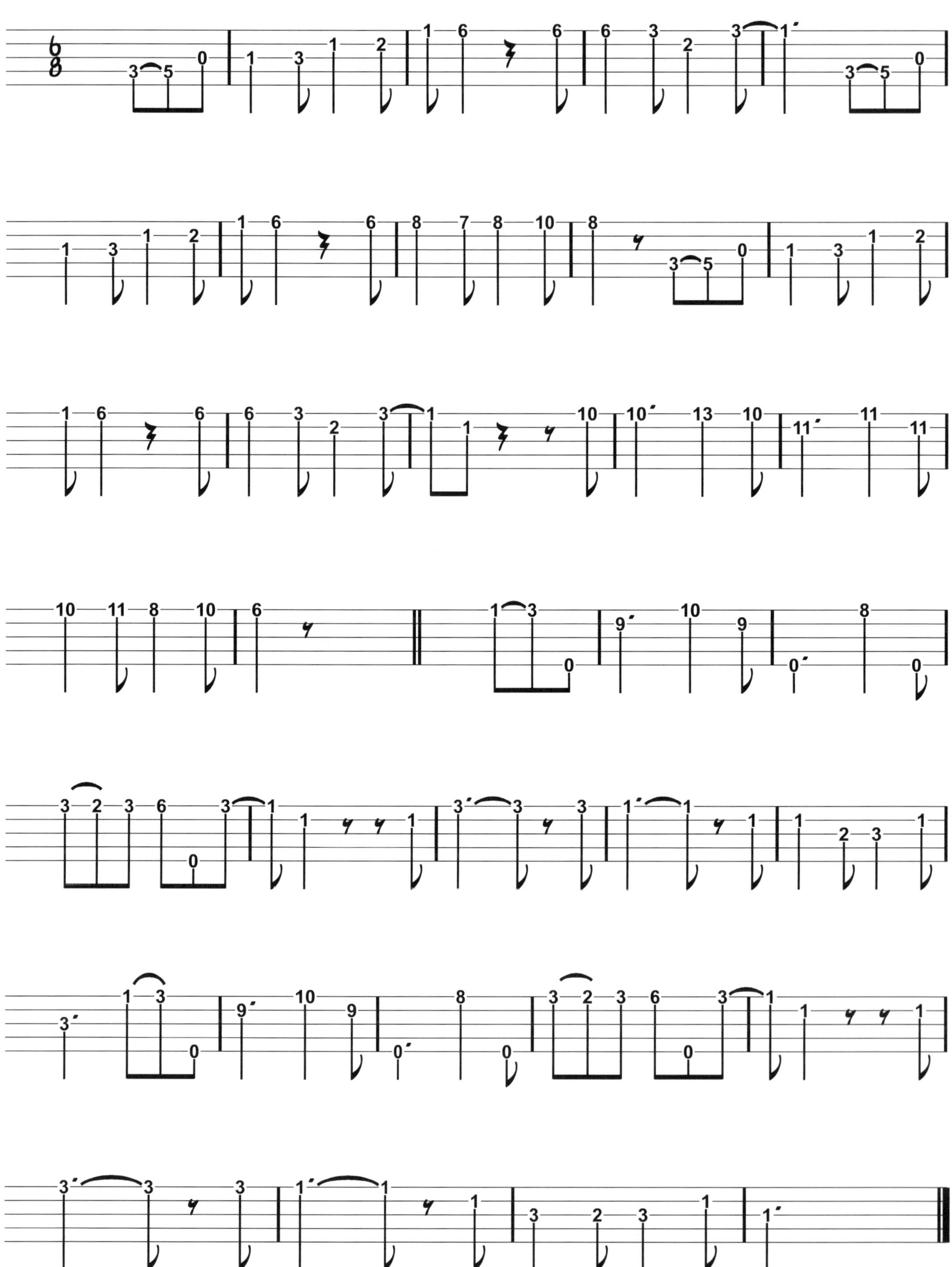

# Essence of Sugar Cane

Slow

1.

2.

Fine

D.C. al Fine

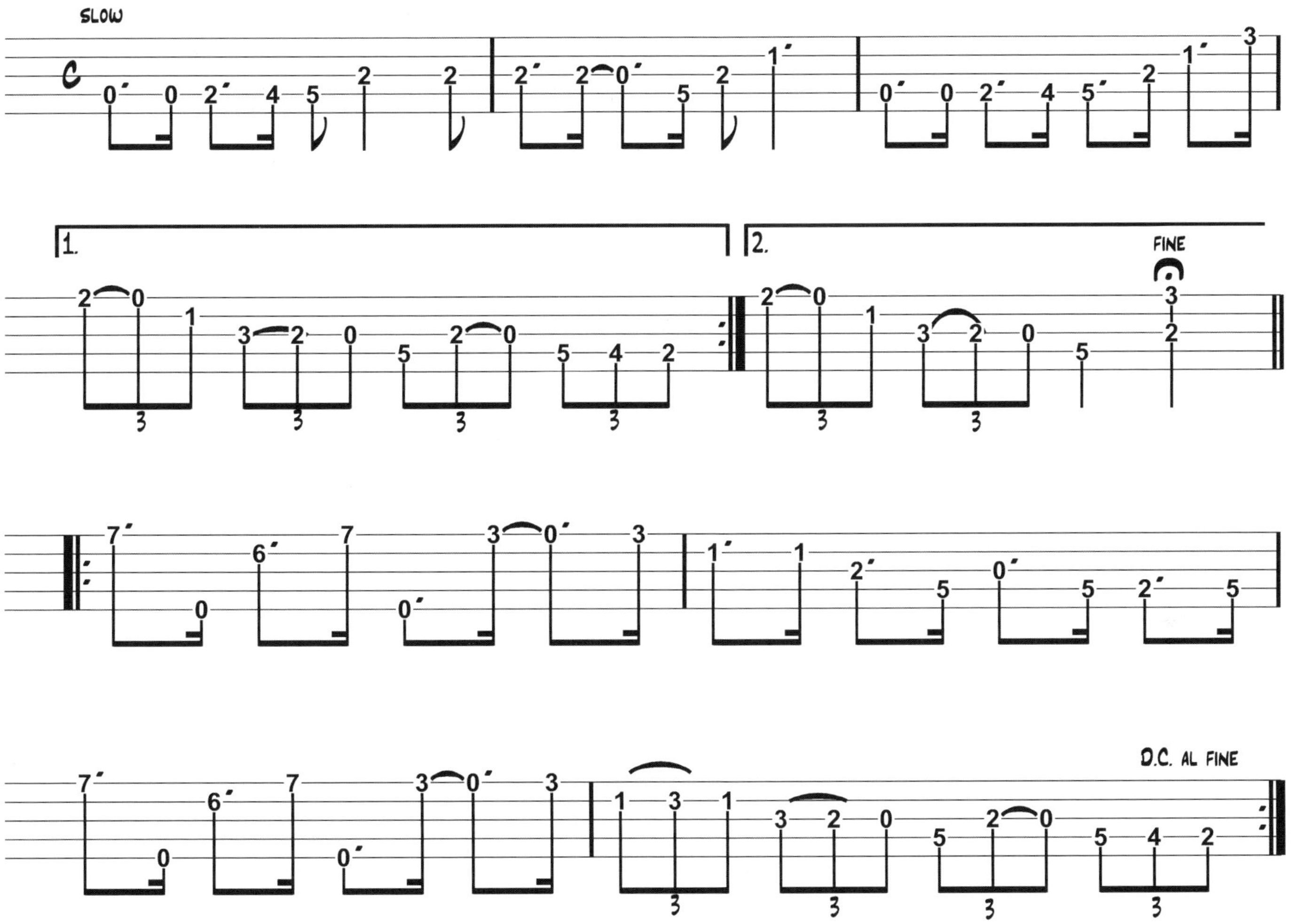

# Fairy Dance

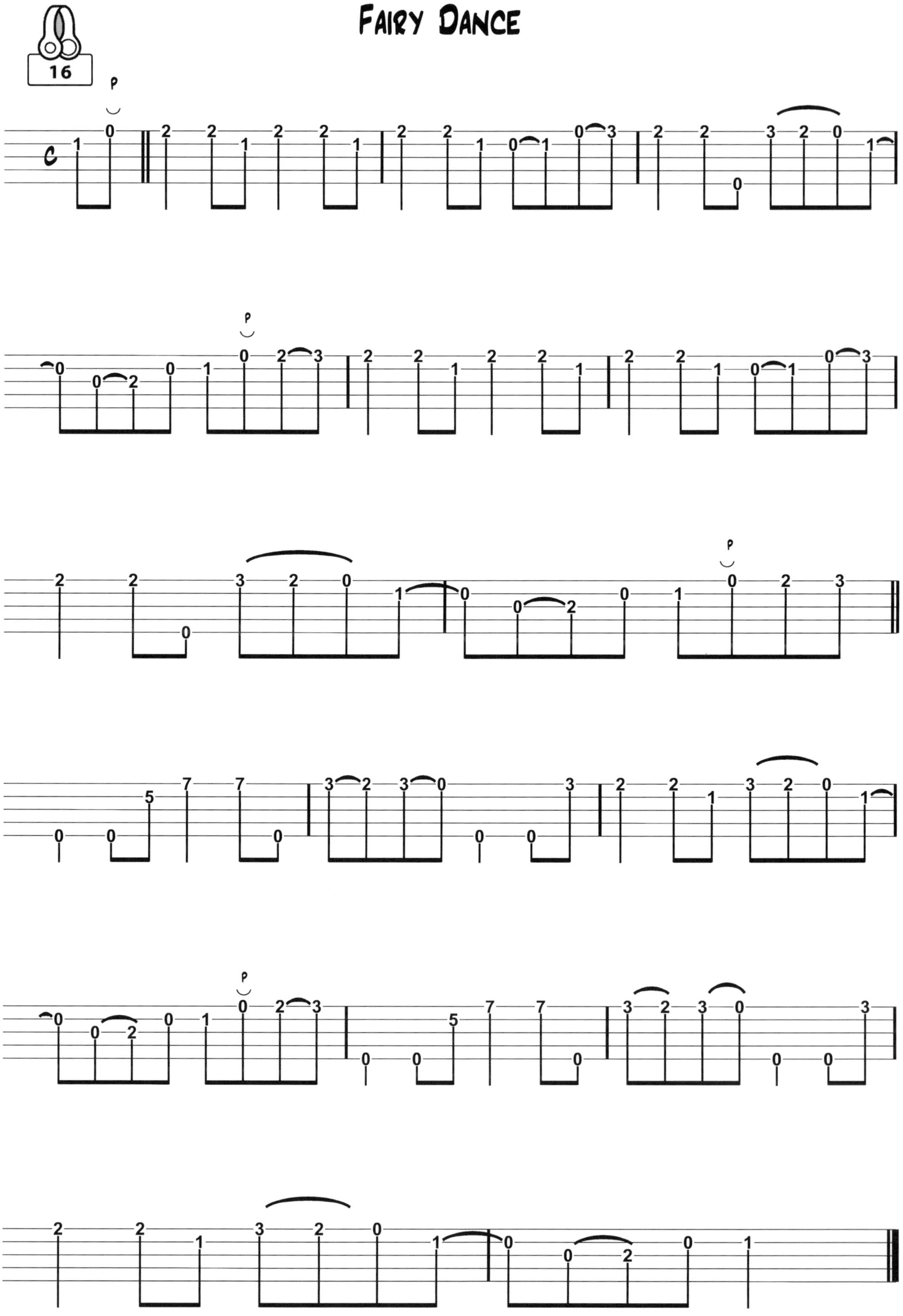

16

# Für Elise

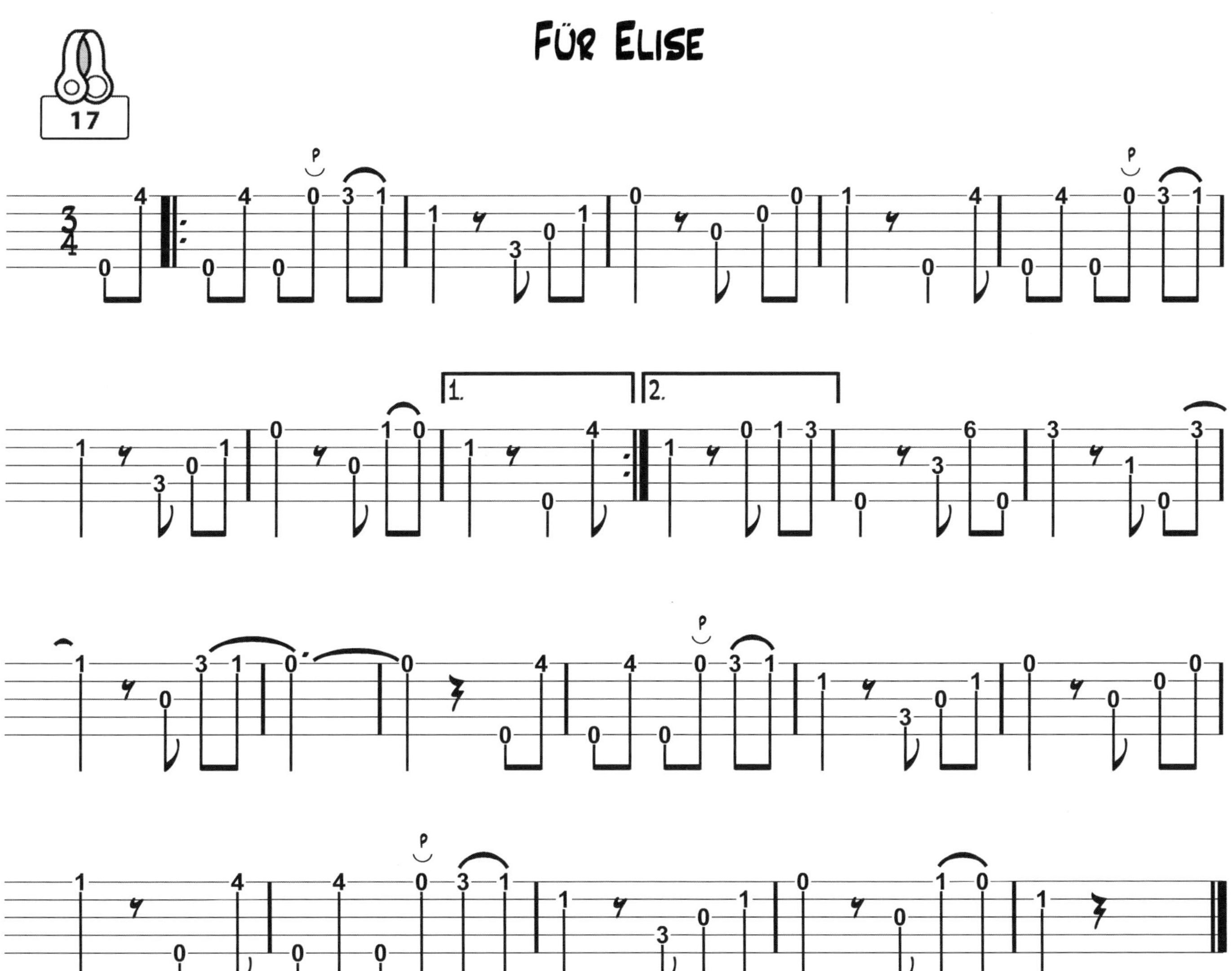

# Genuine Jig

# Golden Slippers

19

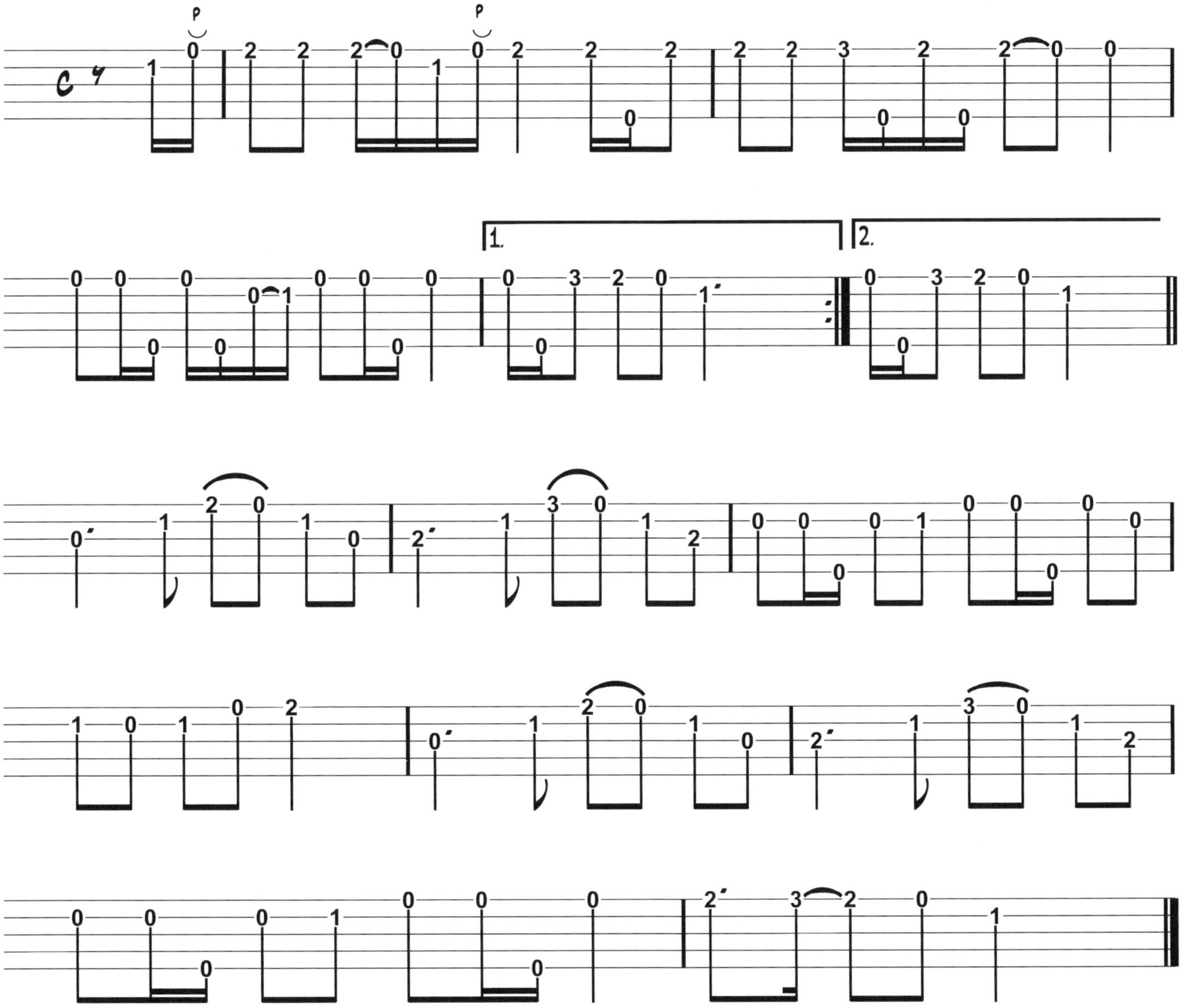

# Grape Vine Twist

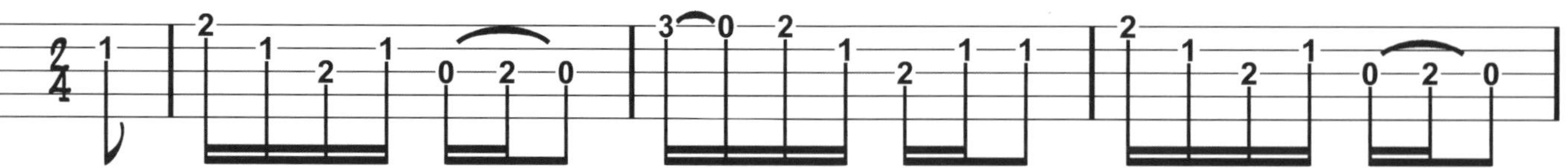

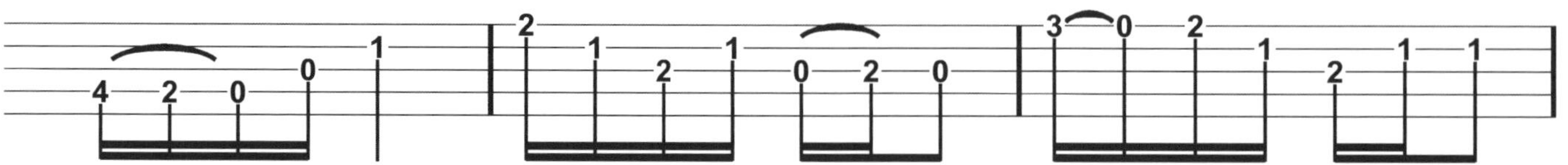

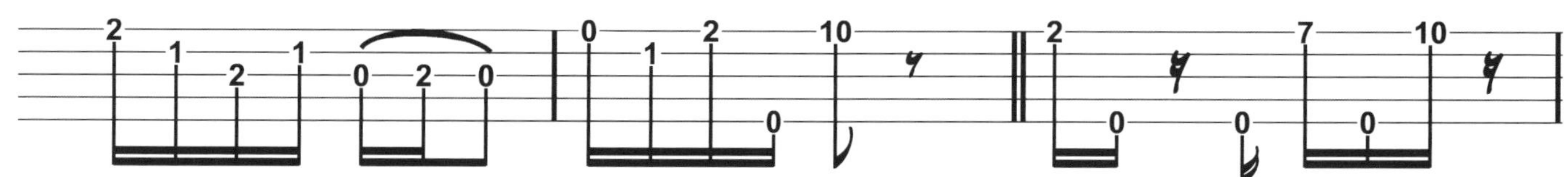

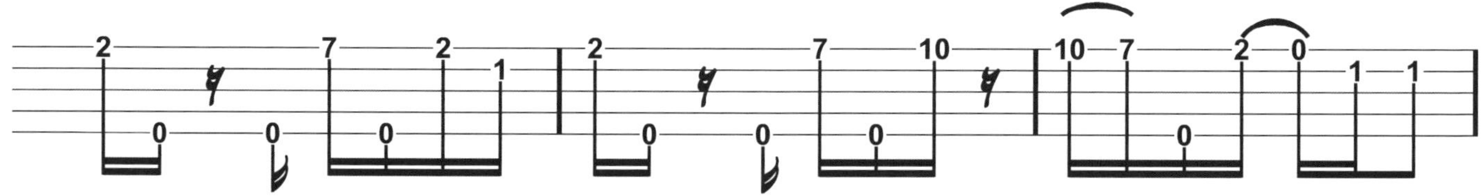

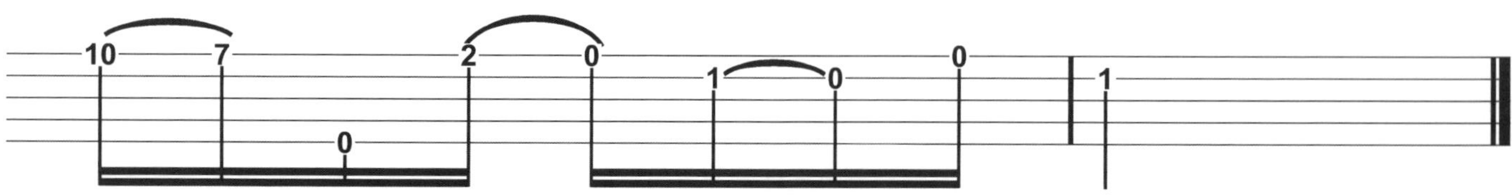

# Harvest Home

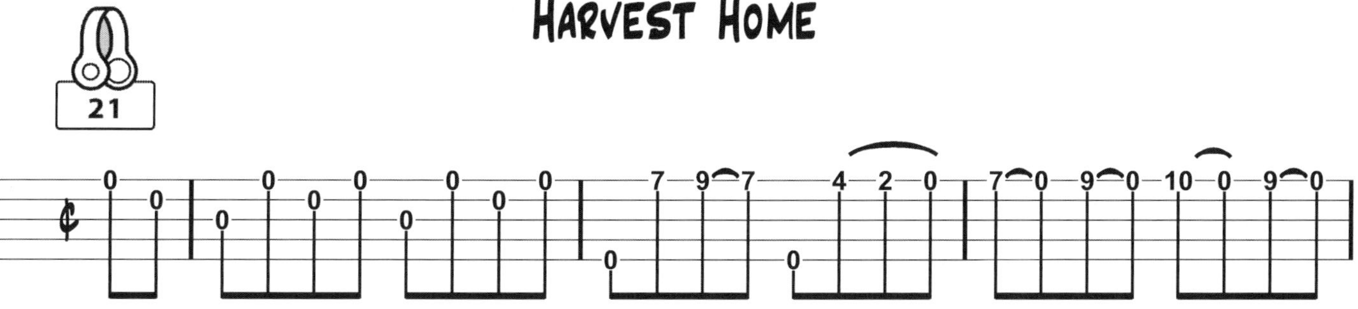


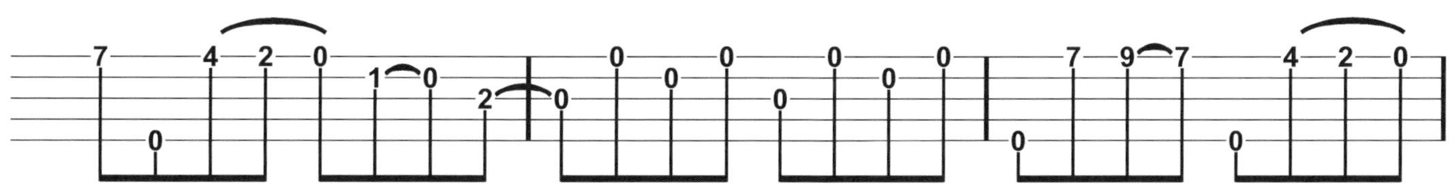

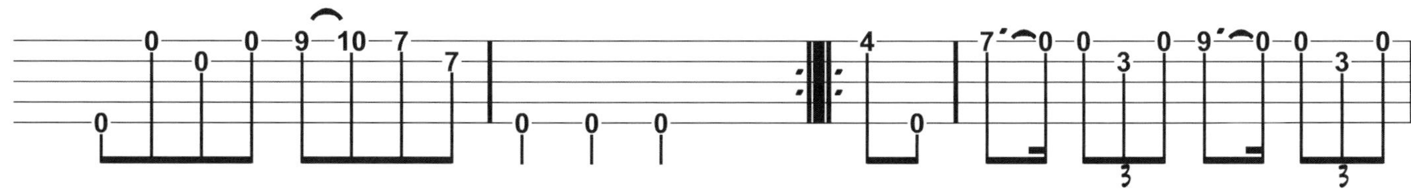

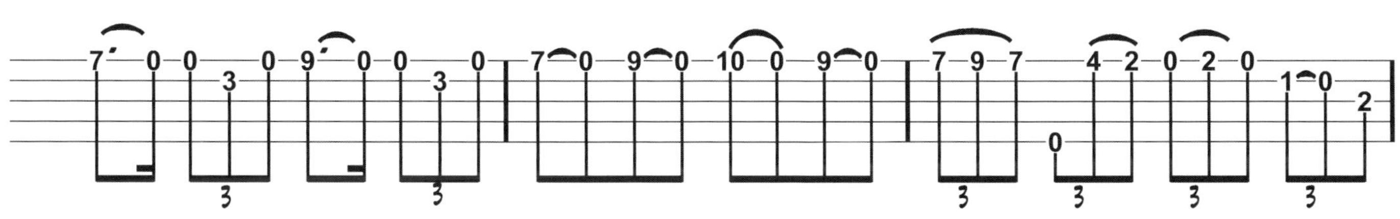

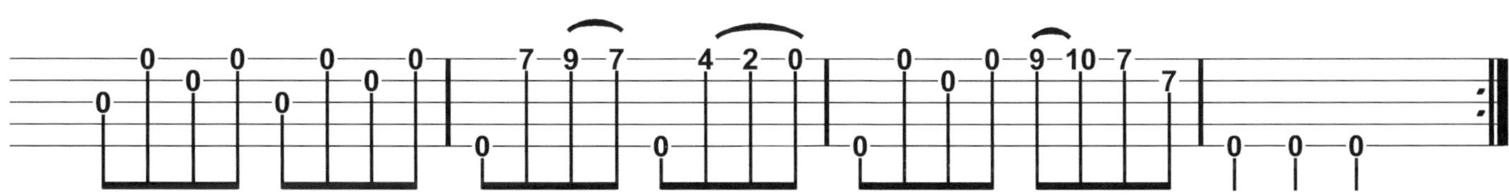

# Hattie Schottische

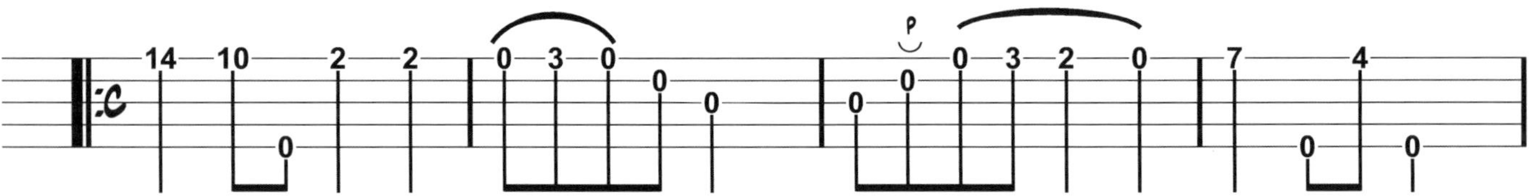

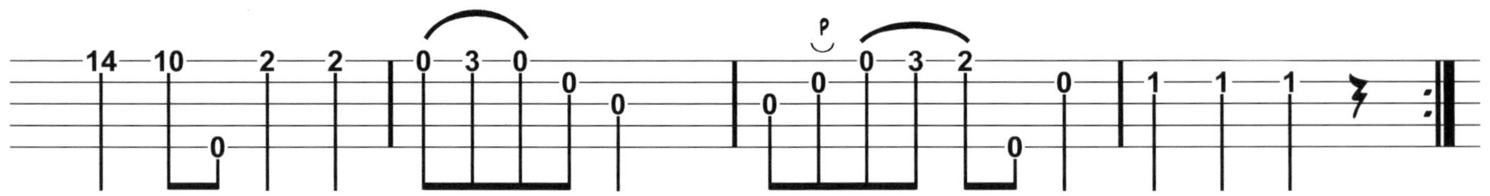

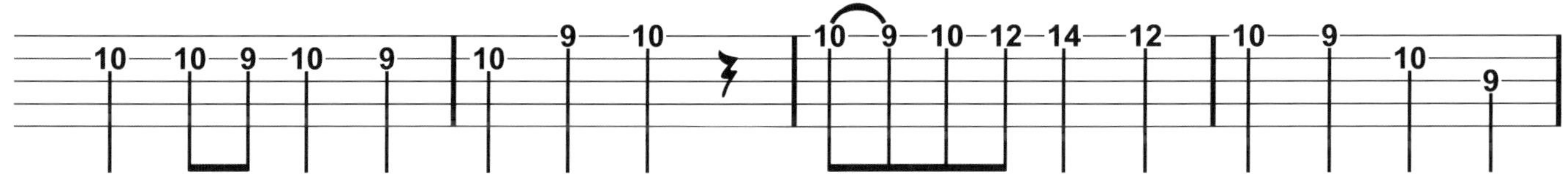

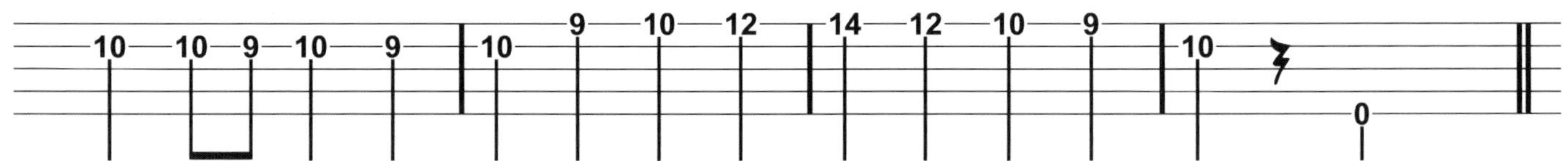

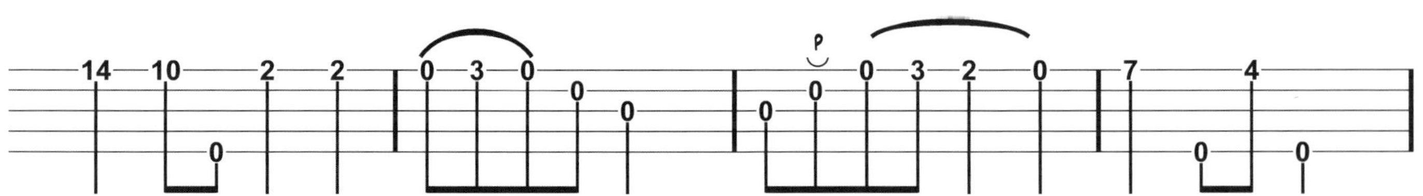

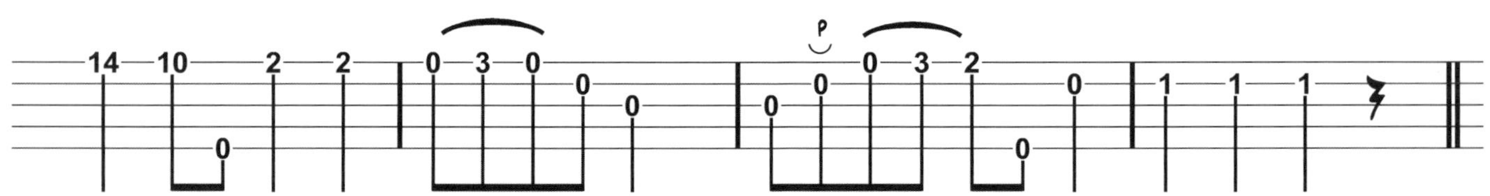

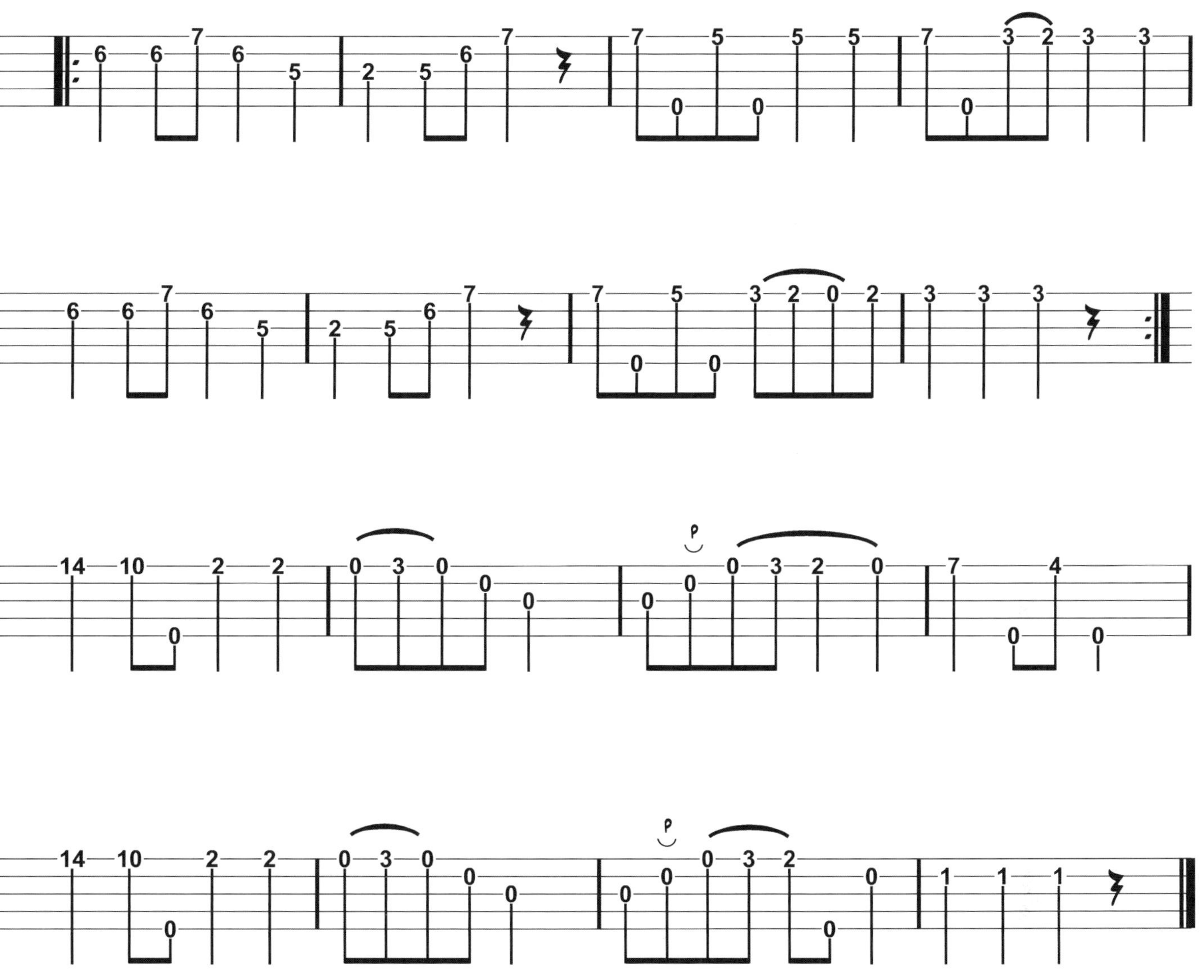

# Haste to the Wedding

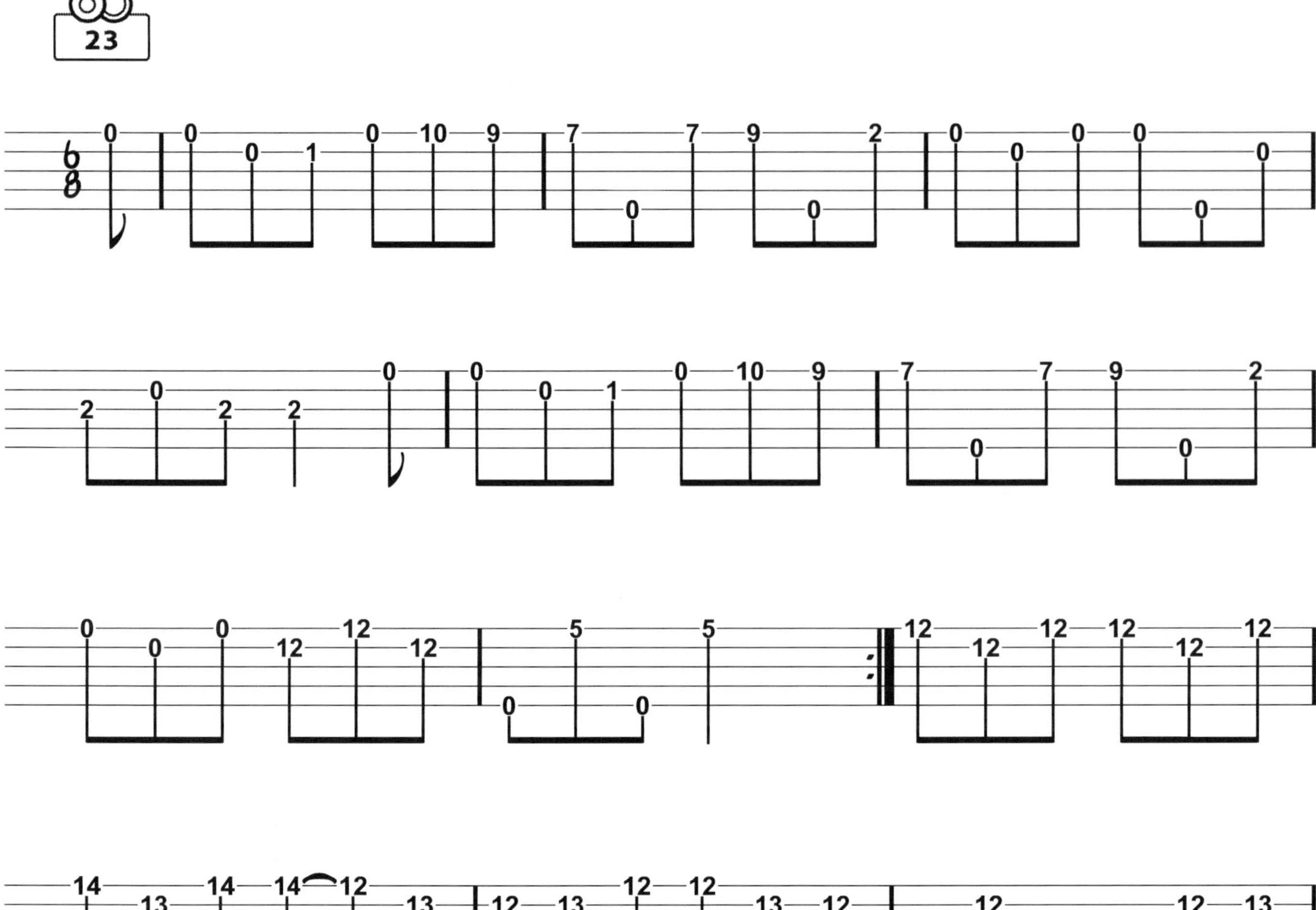

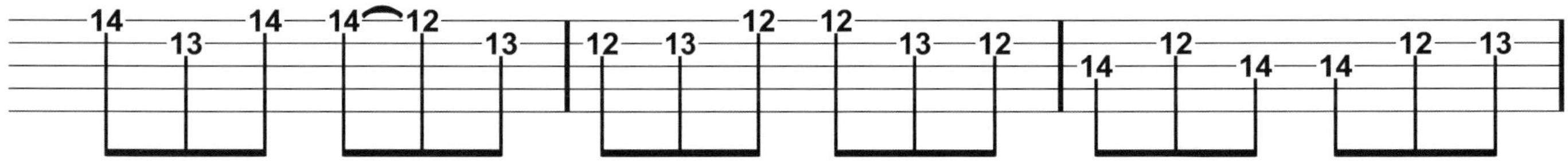

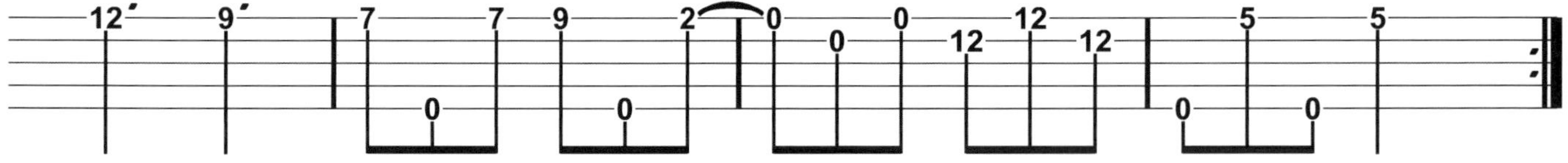

# Isabella Doane Schottische

24

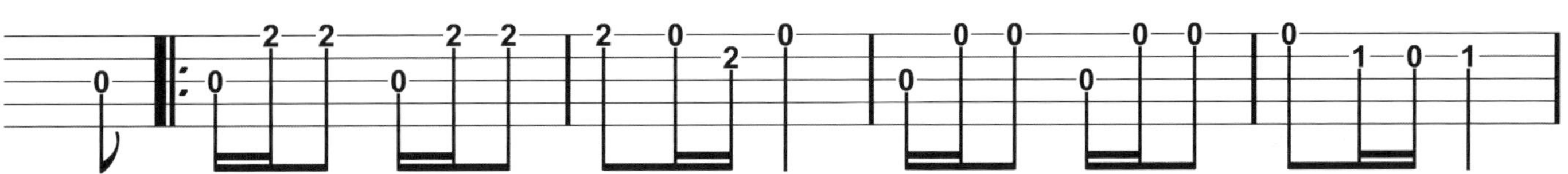

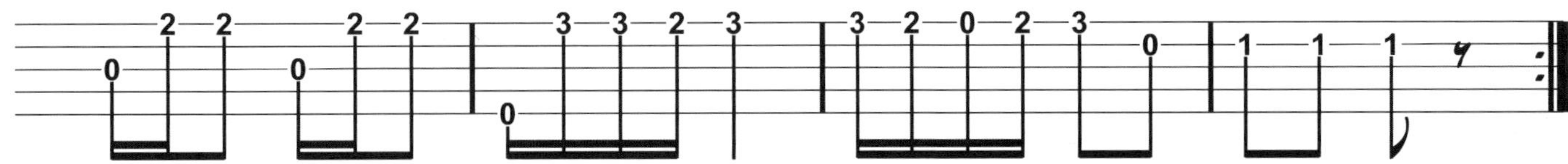

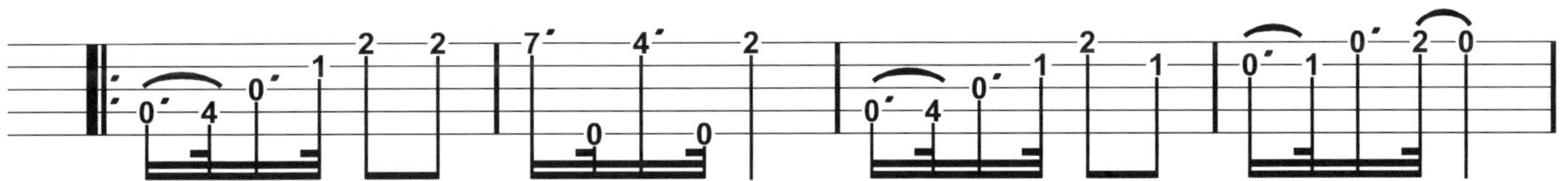

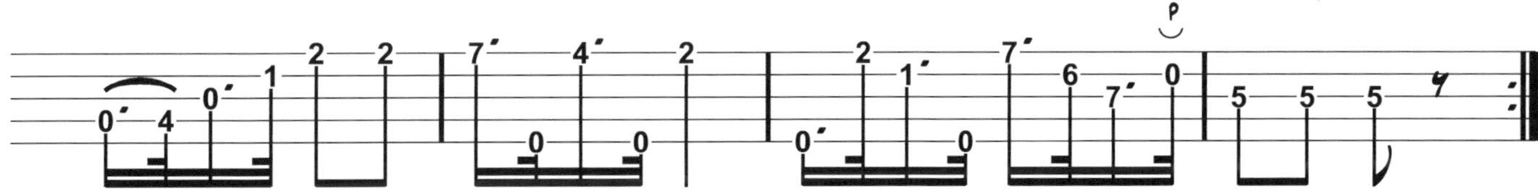

# KILKENNY HORNPIPE

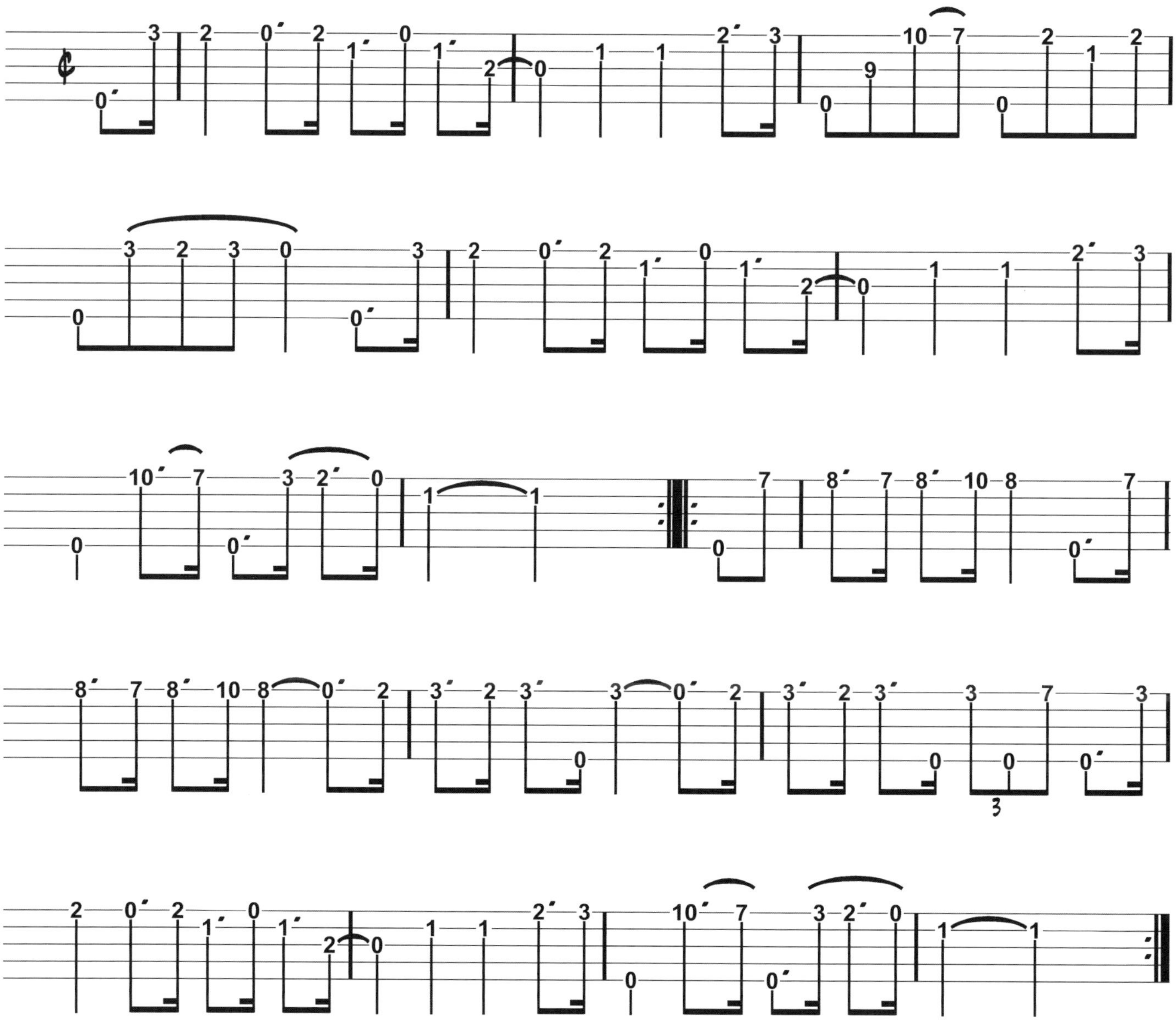

# Lincoln's Hornpipe

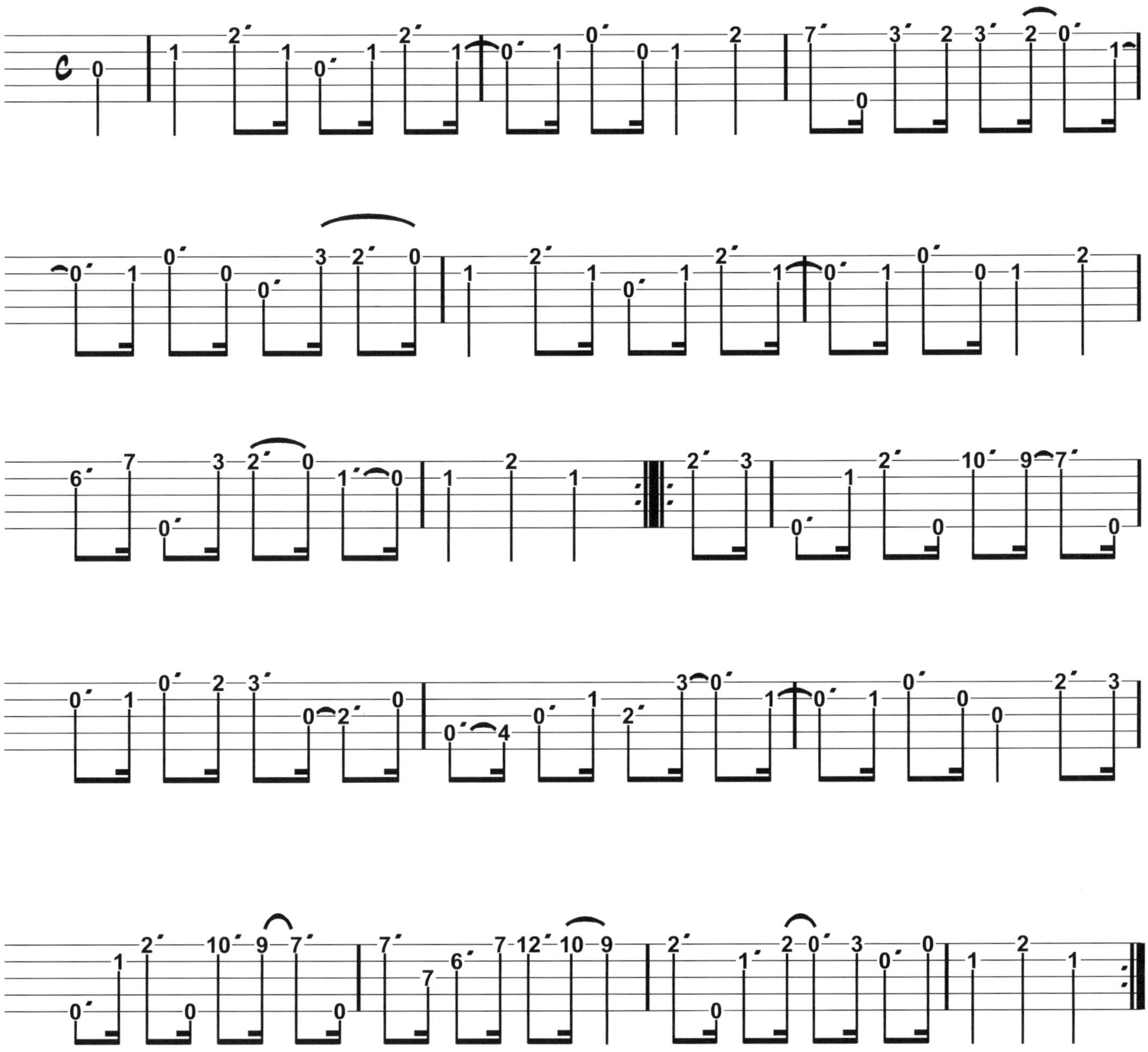

# Long Tail Blue

27

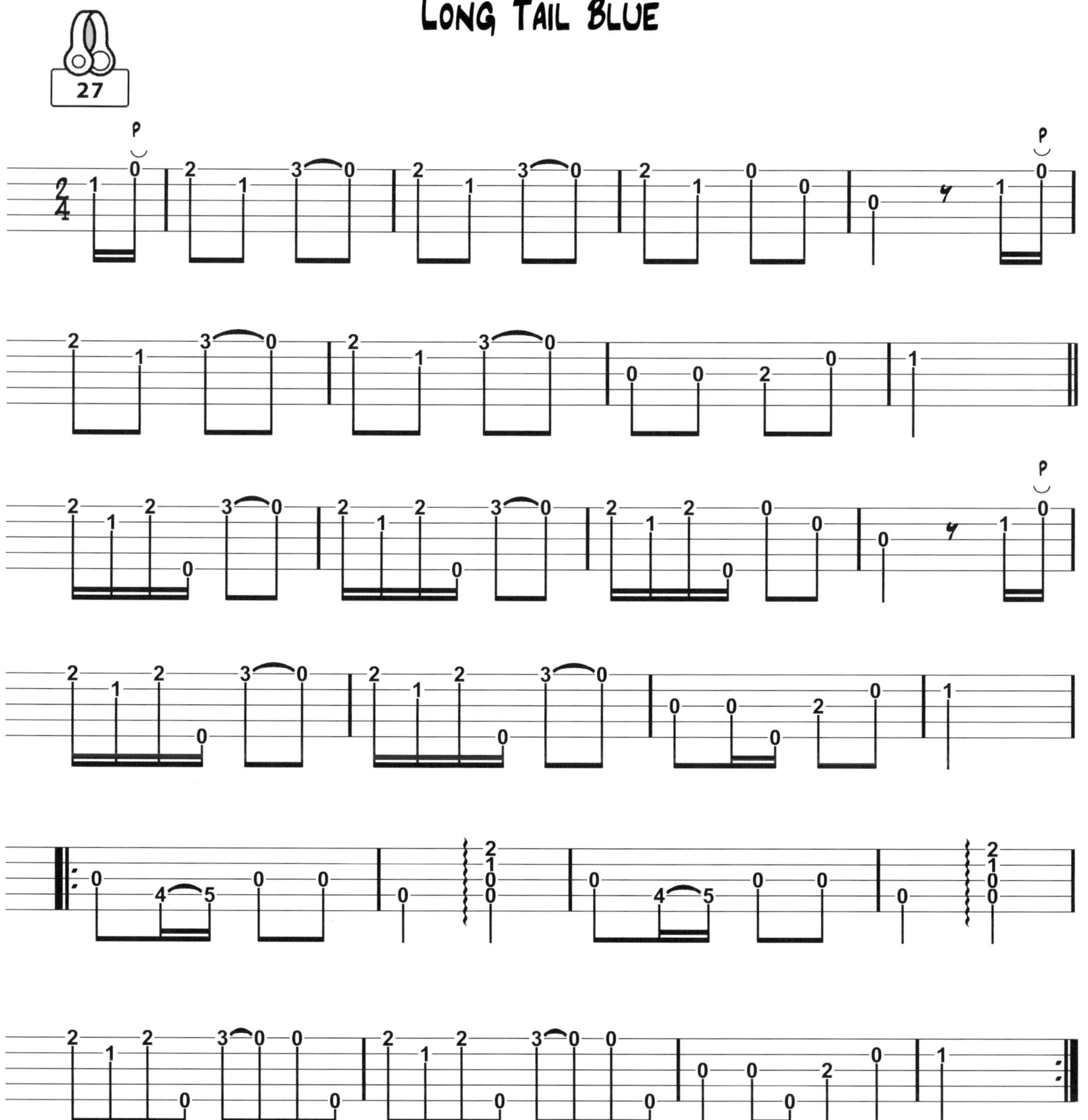

# Minstrel's Fancy-Clog

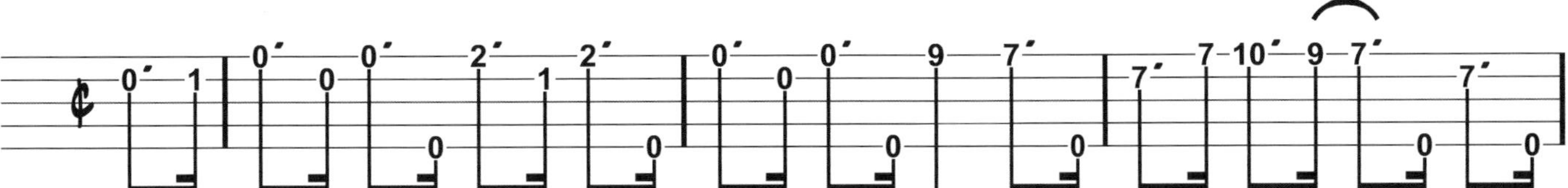

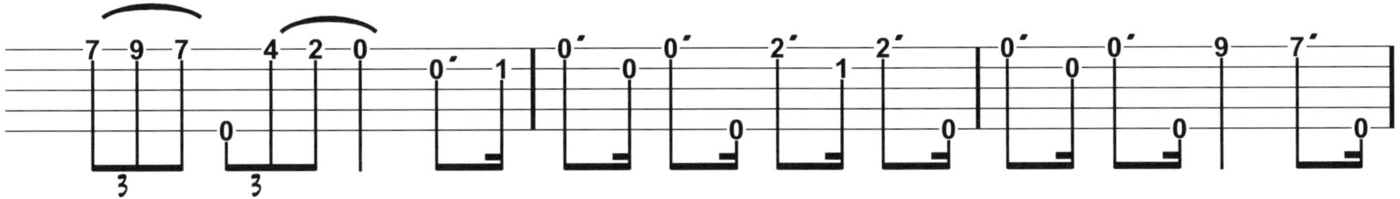

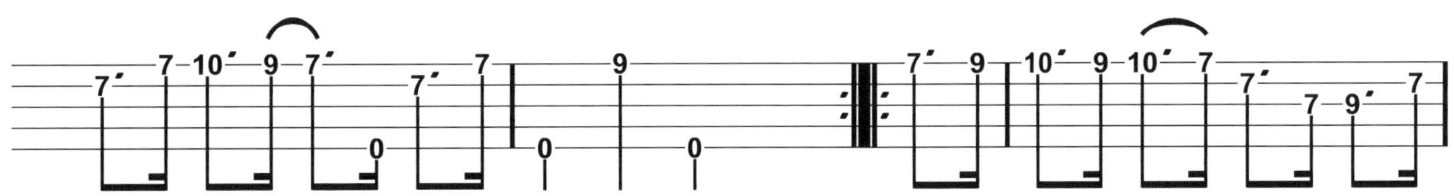

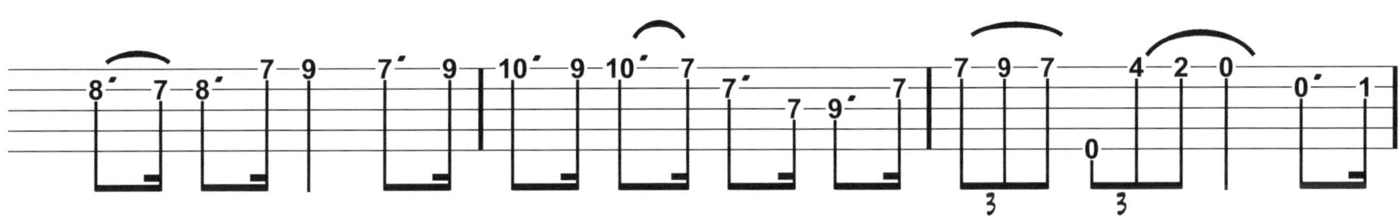

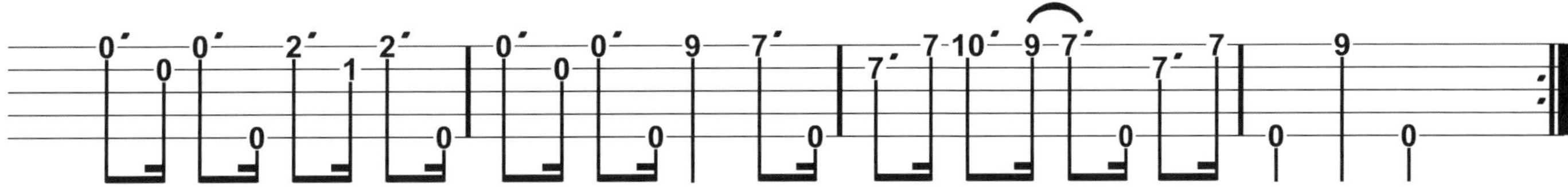

# Miss Daly's Jig

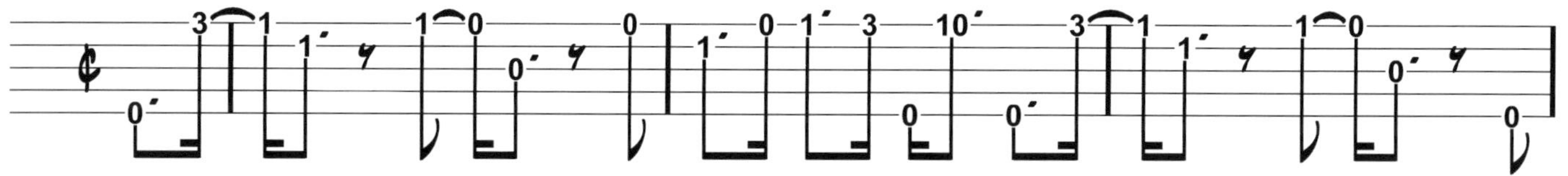

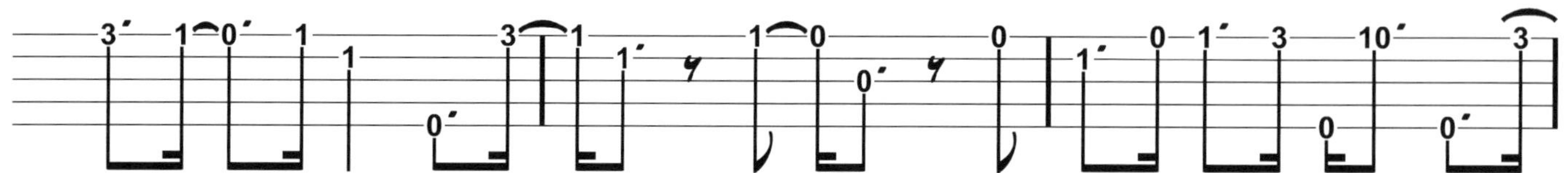

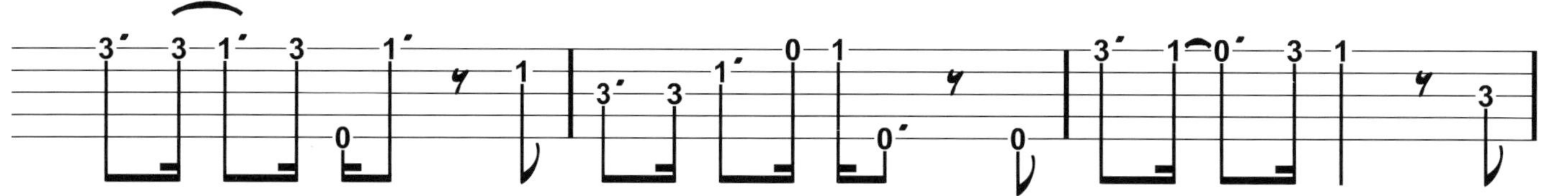

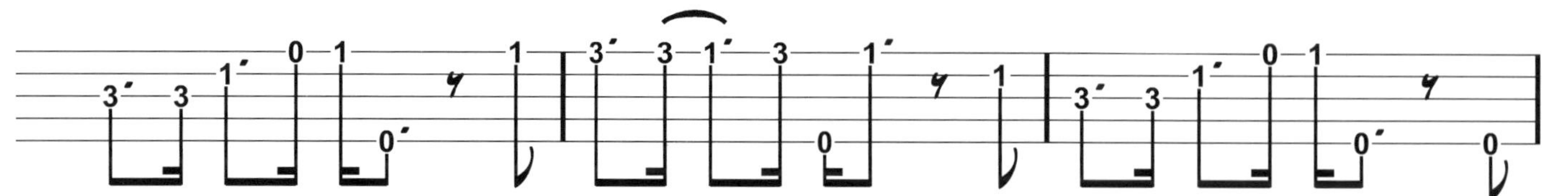

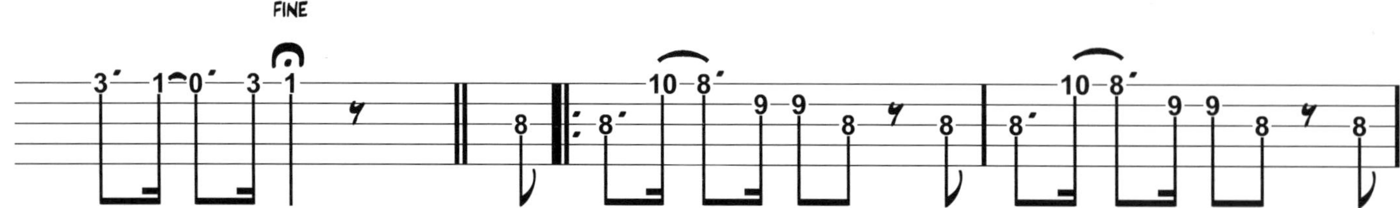

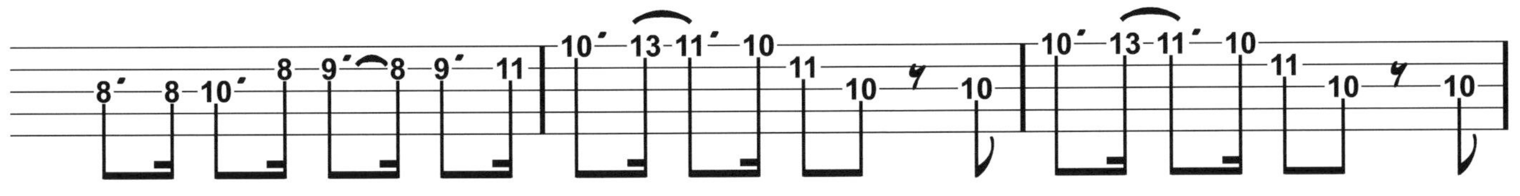

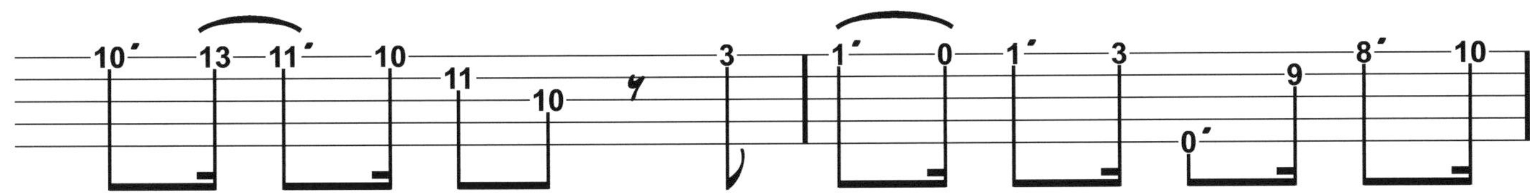

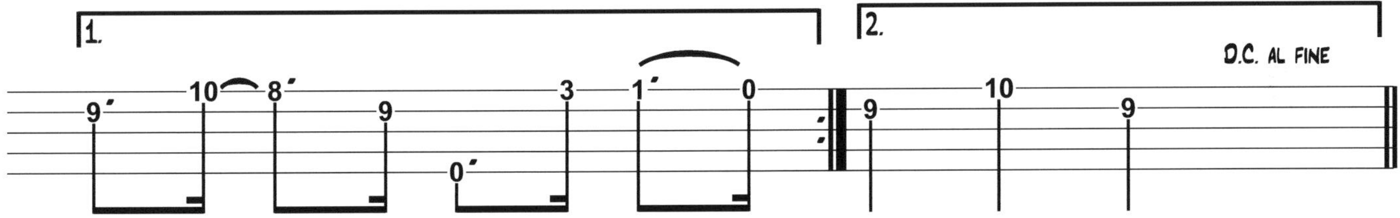
1.
2.
D.C. AL FINE

30

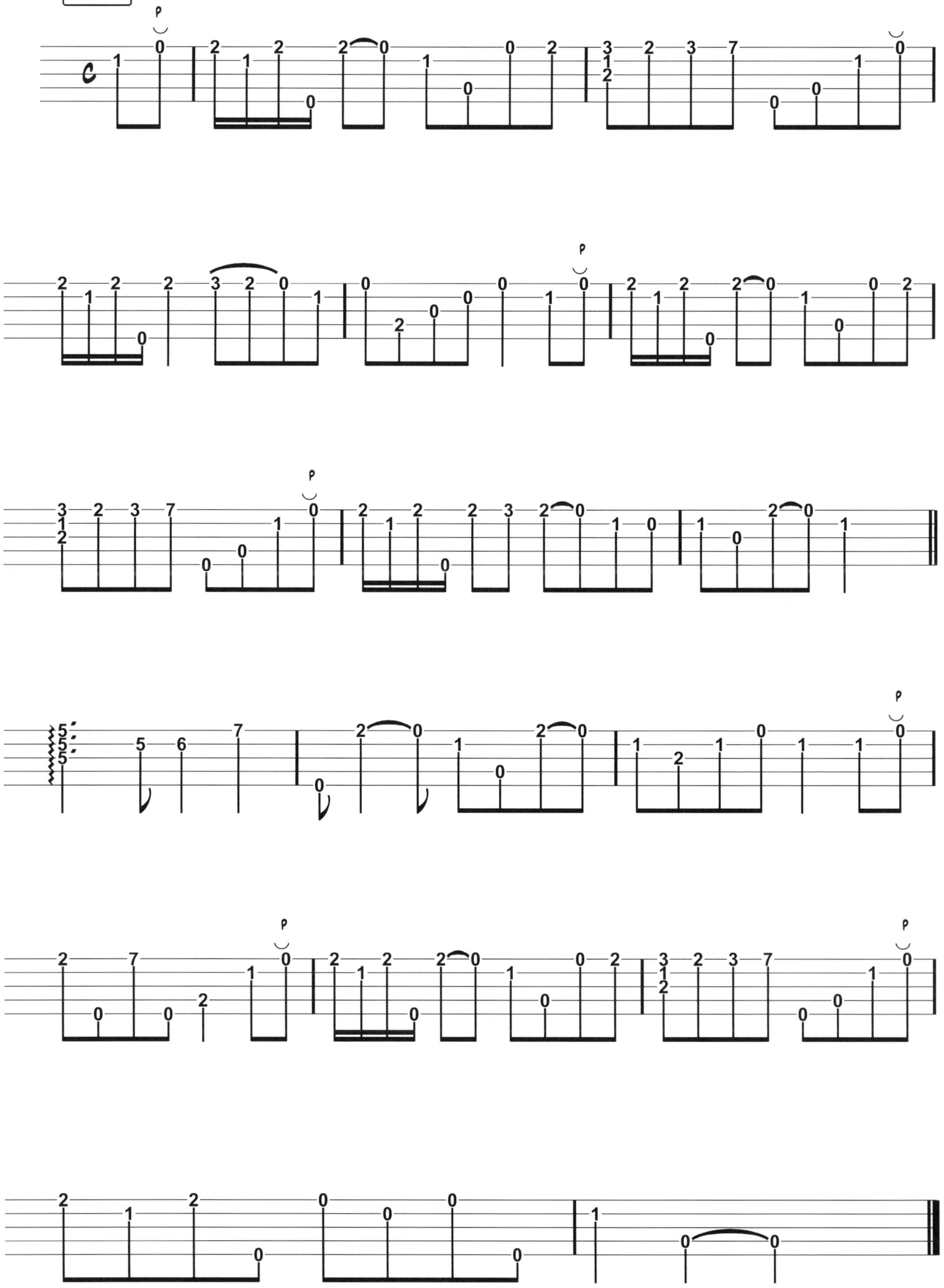

# Mrs. Francis Wemyss

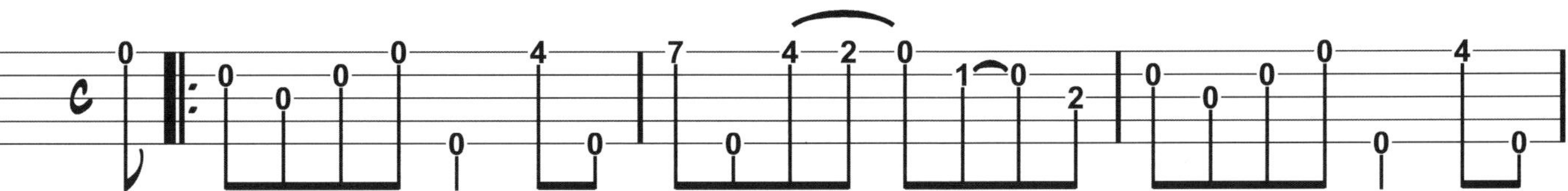

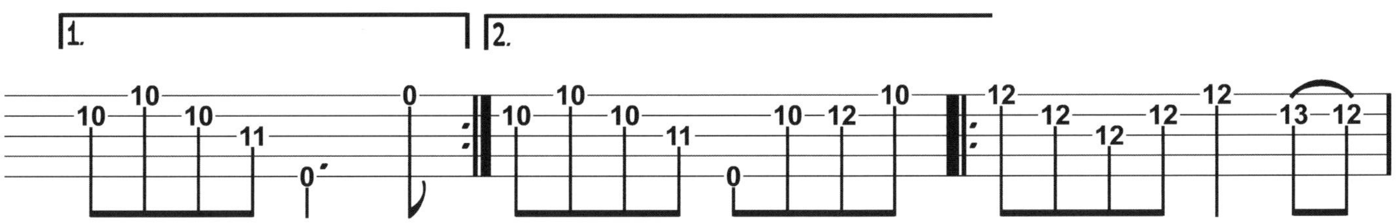


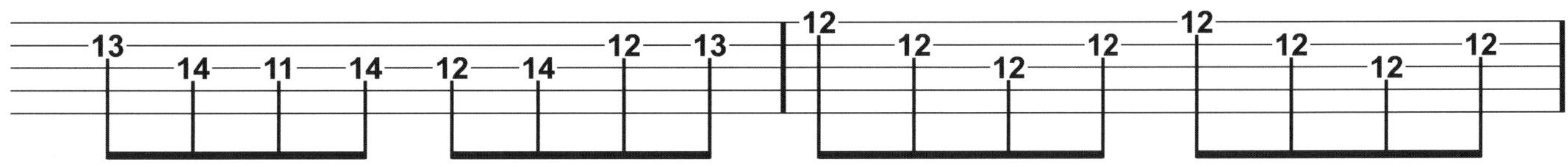

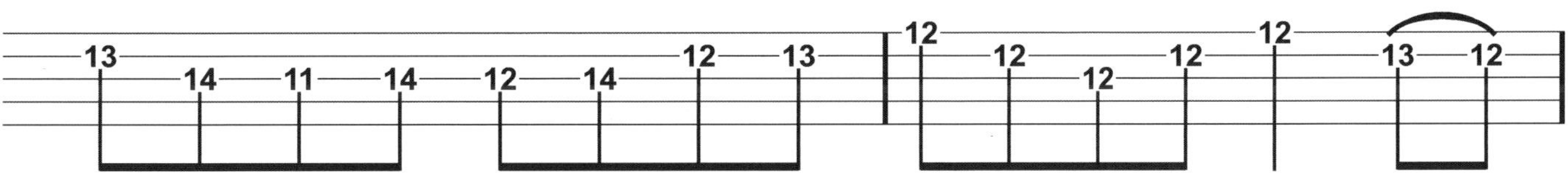

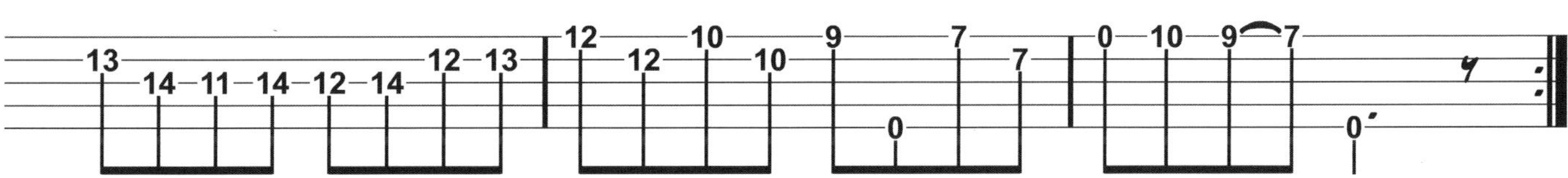

# Nighttime Lament

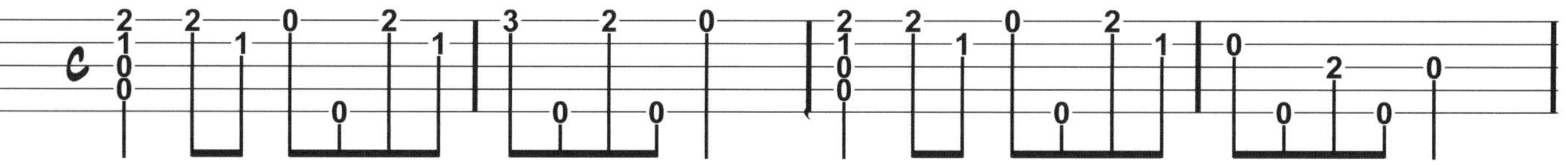

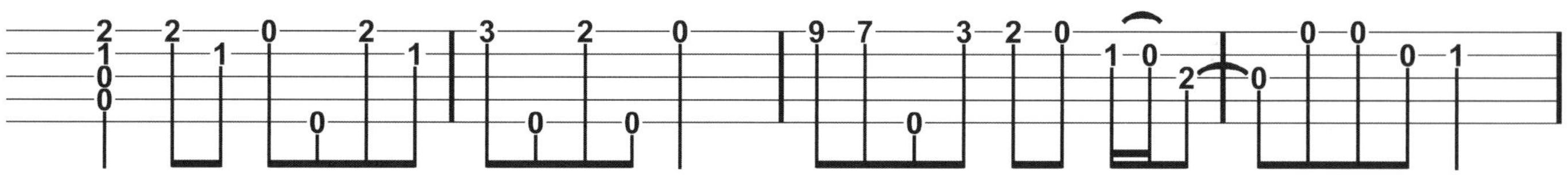

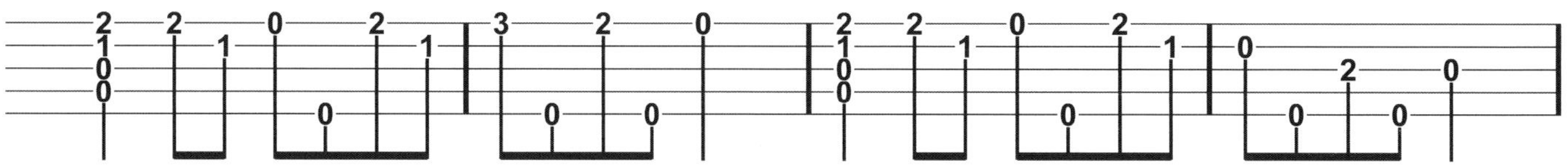

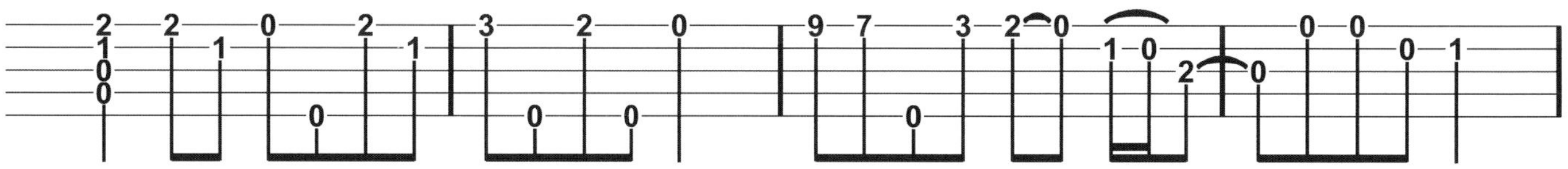

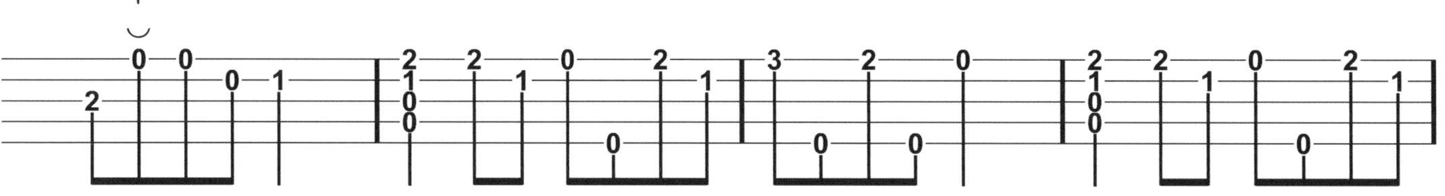

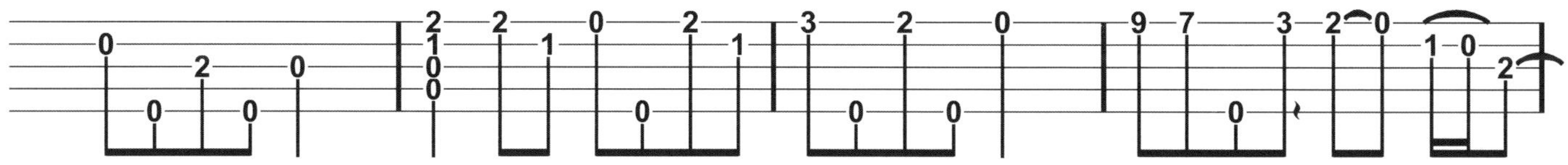

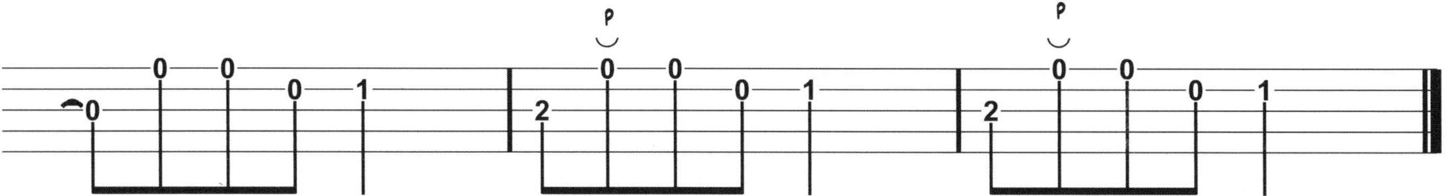

# O Little Town of Bethlehem

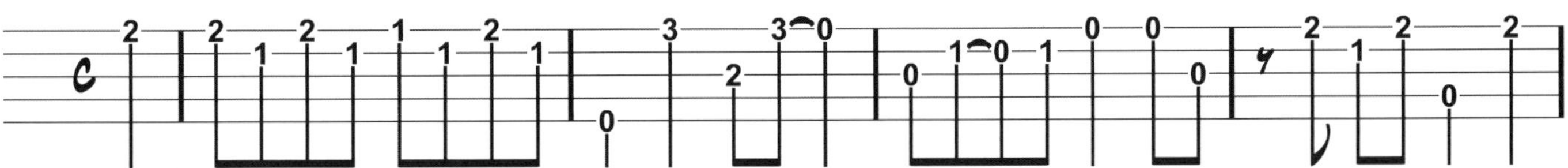

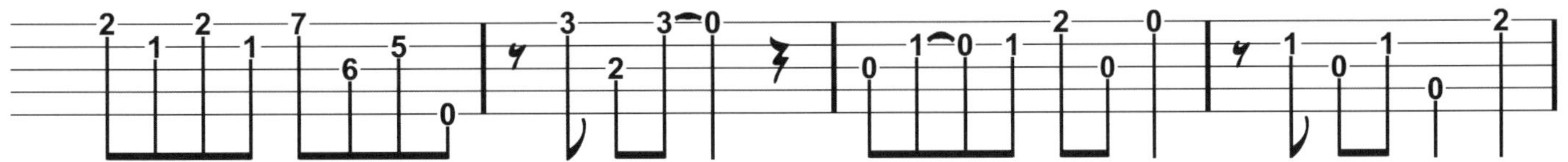

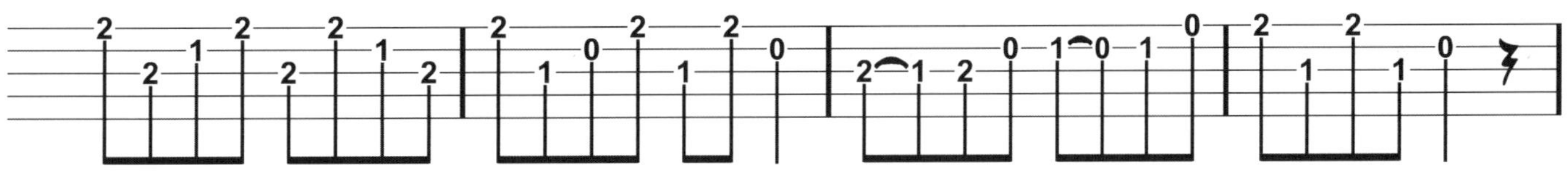

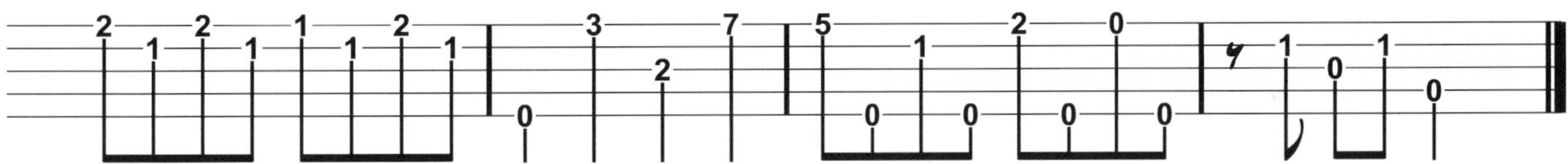

# Old Tare River

34

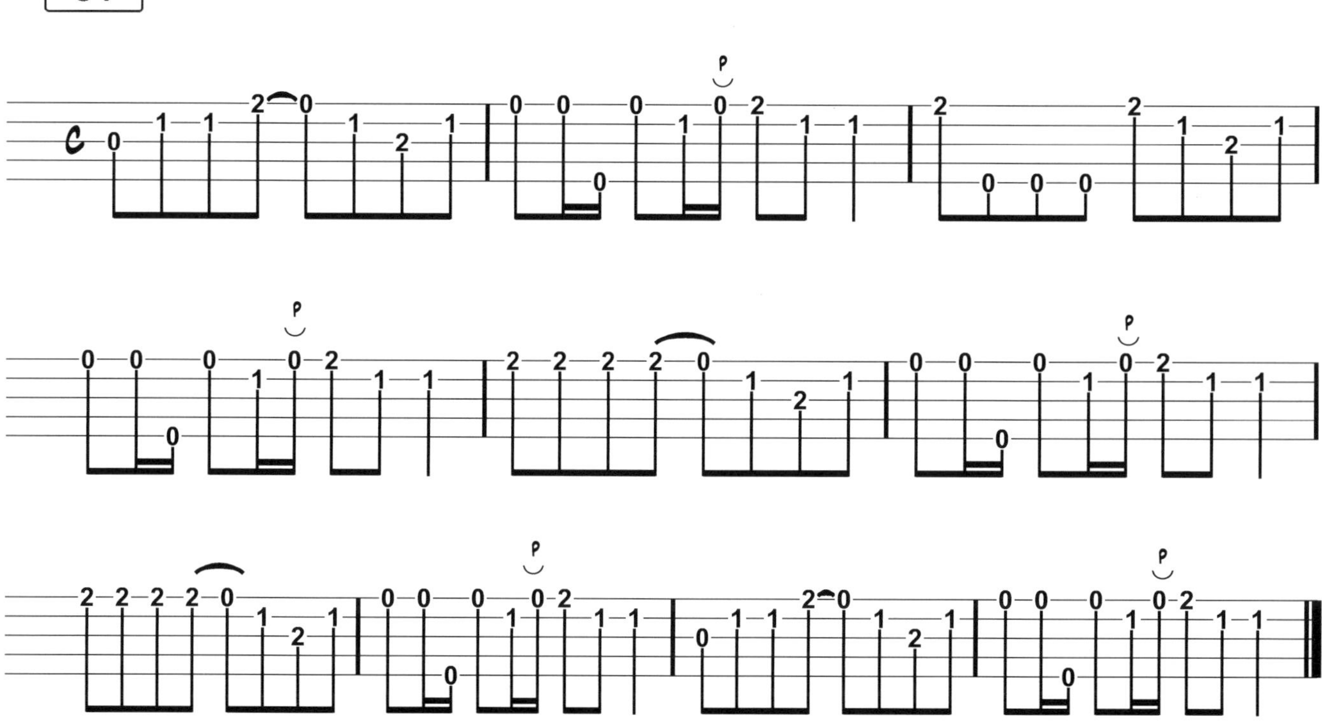

# The Bonnie Blue Flag

35

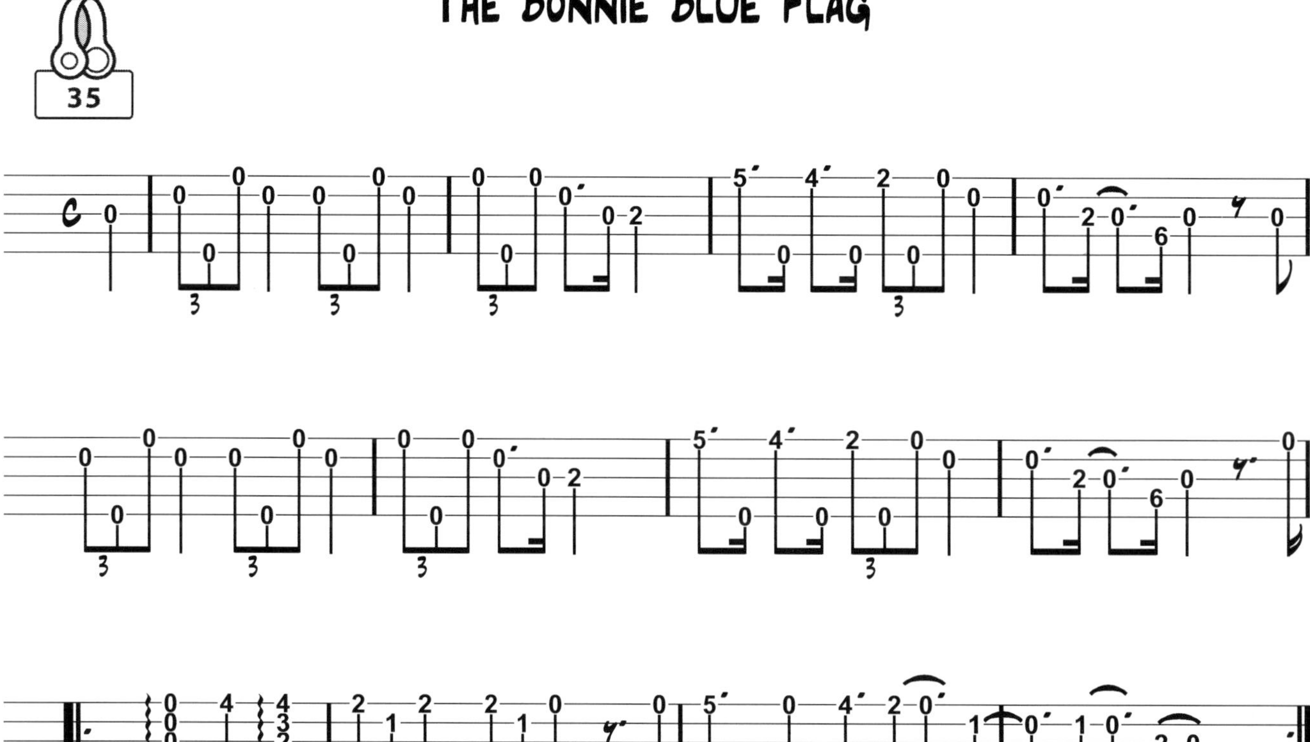

# Oyster Sally

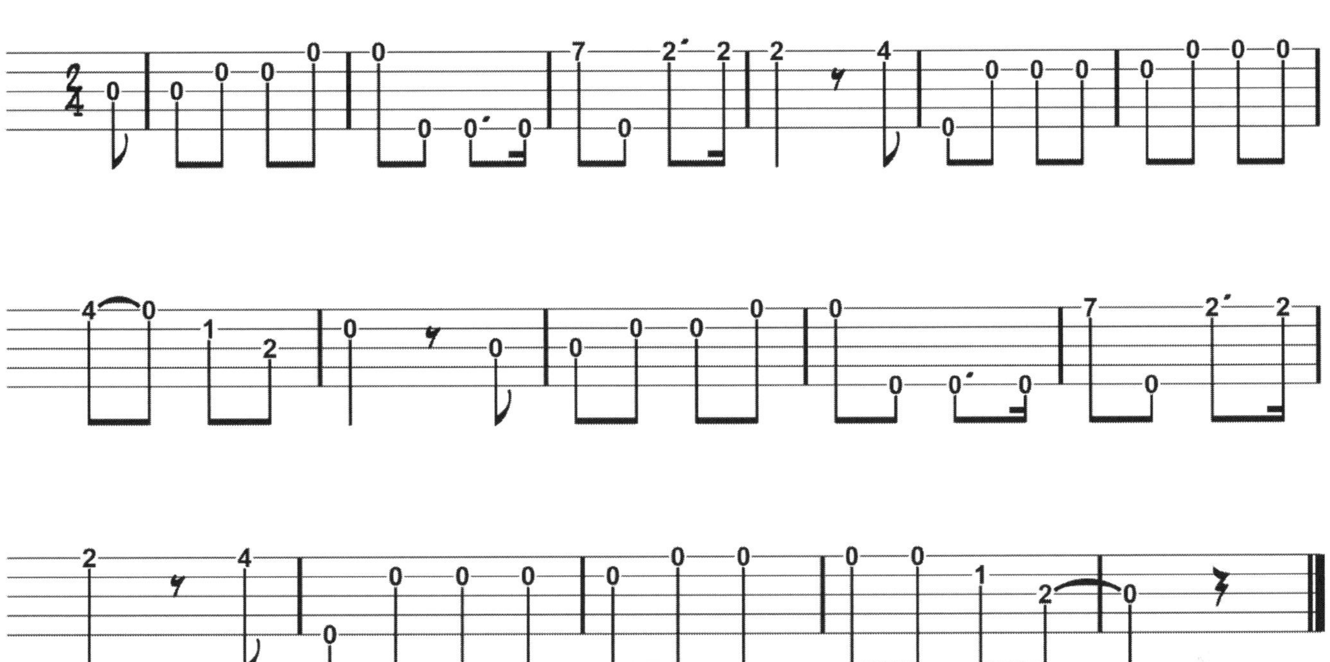

# Pompey Ran Away

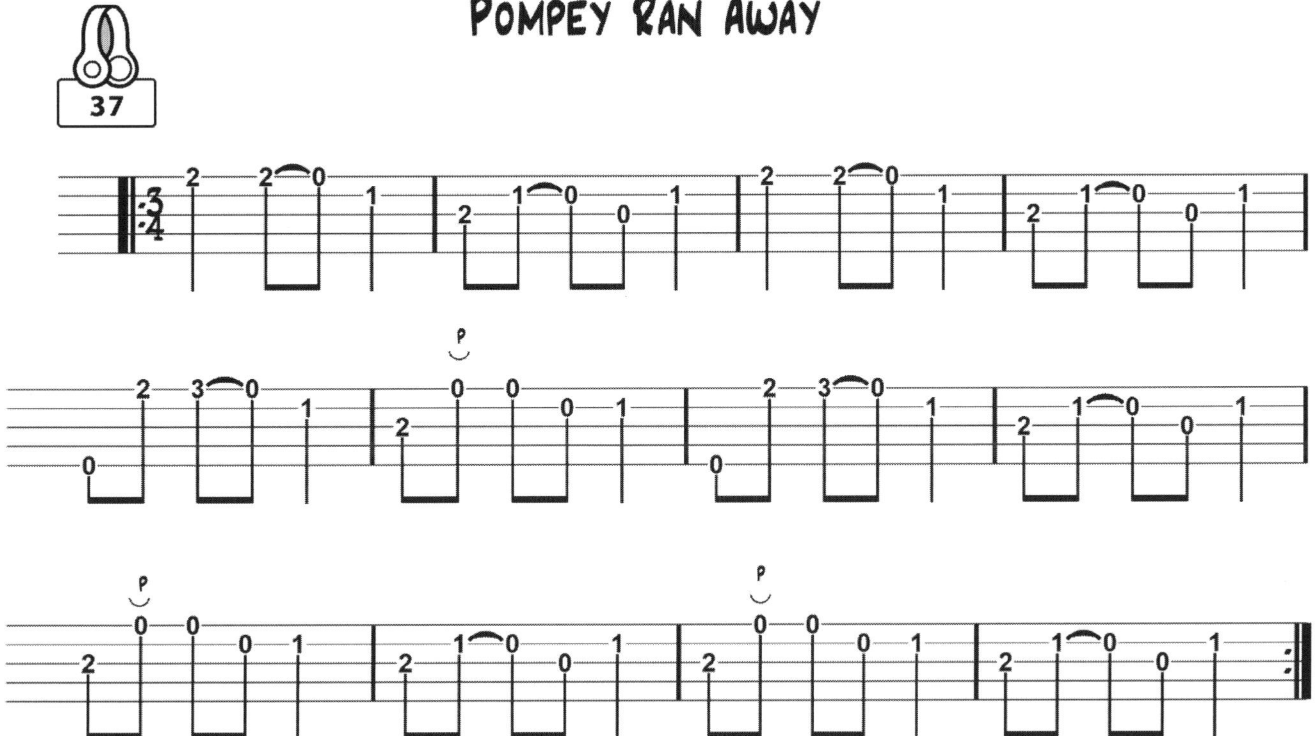

# Rattle the Cash Jig

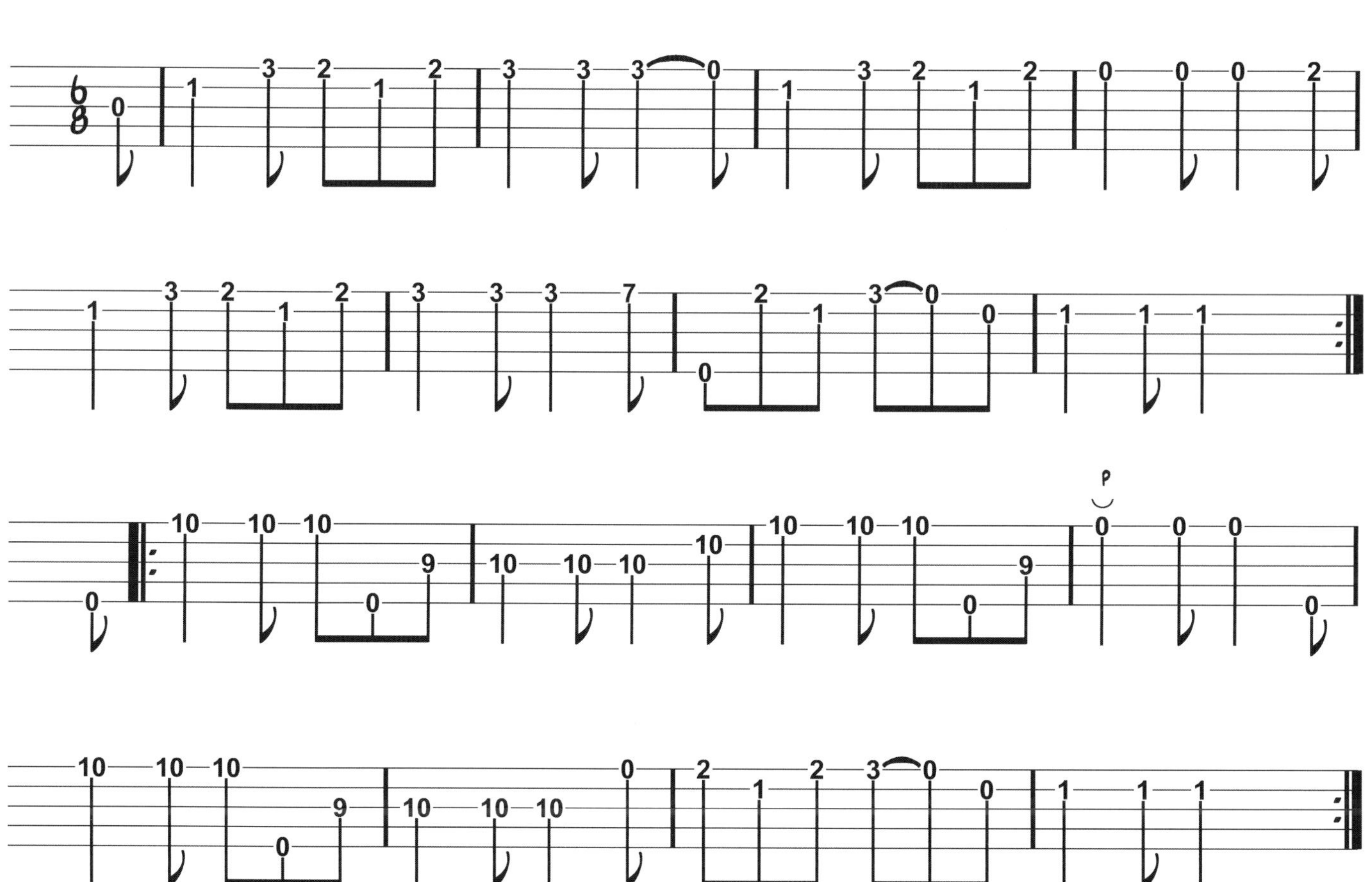

# Rose of Alabama

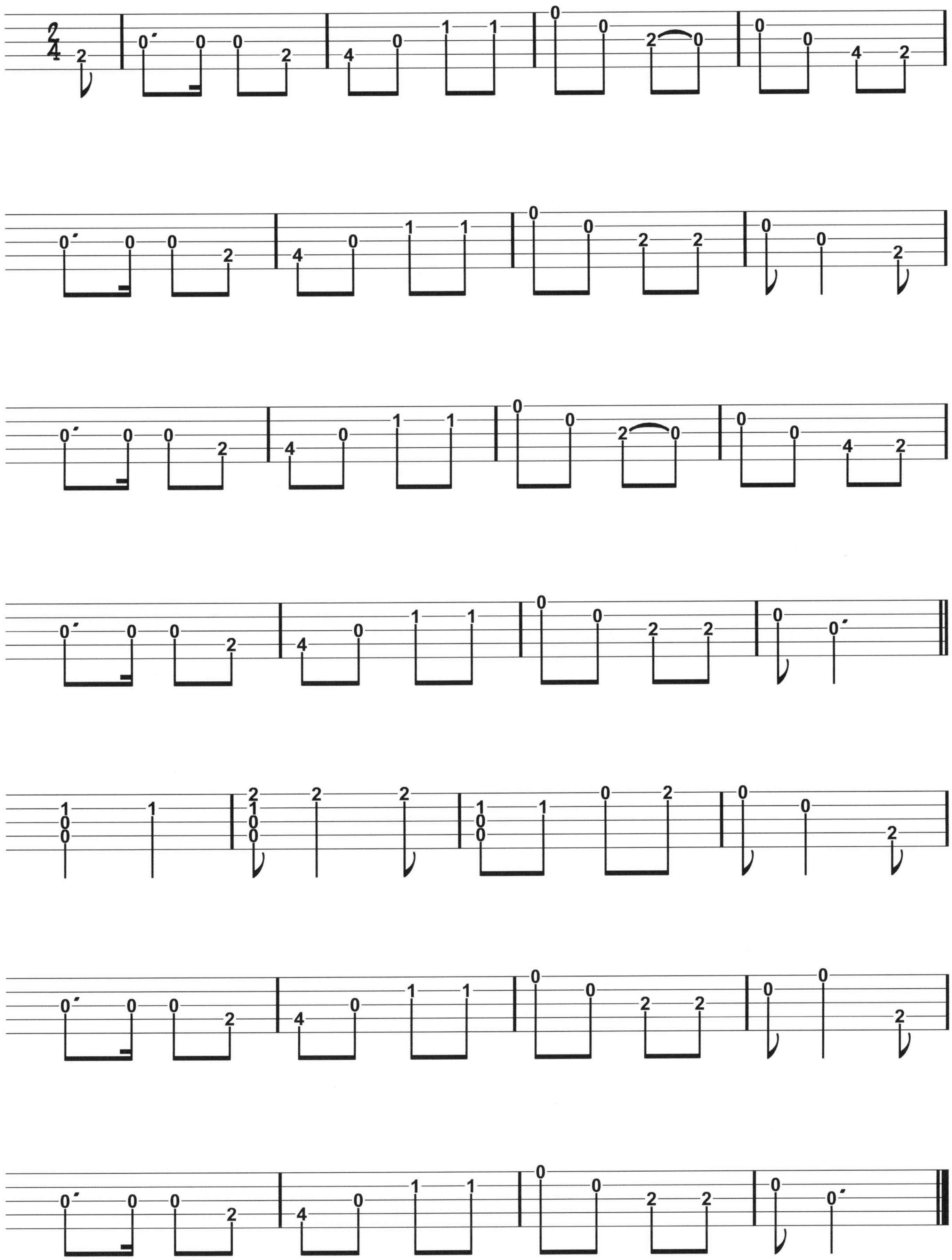

# Rustic Dance

Fine

D.C. al Fine

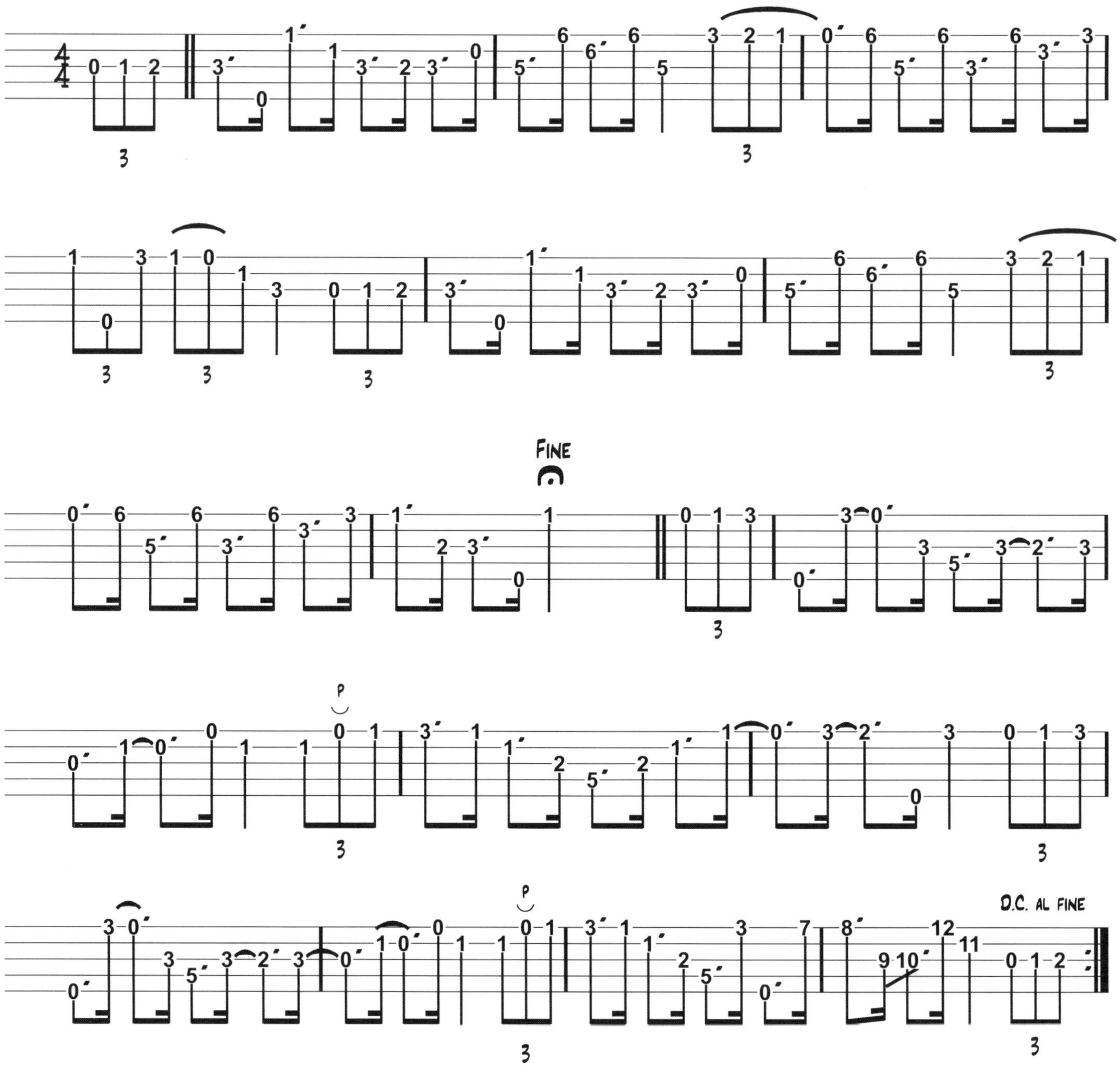

# Sam's Opinion

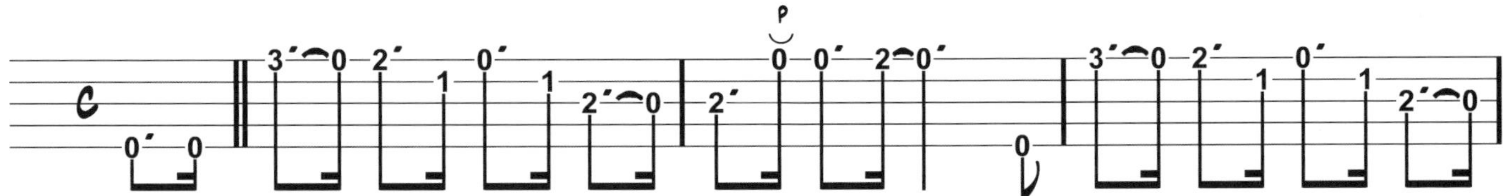

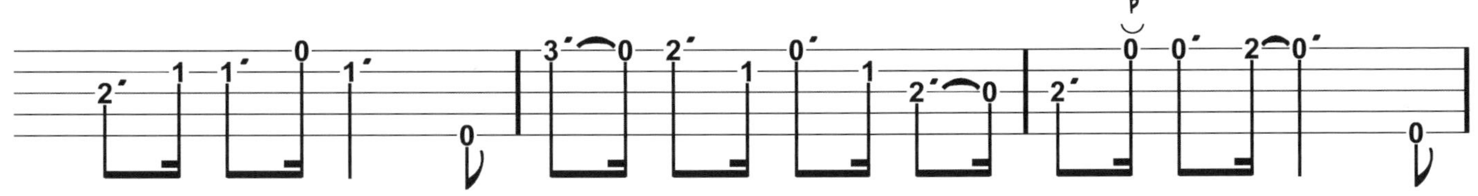

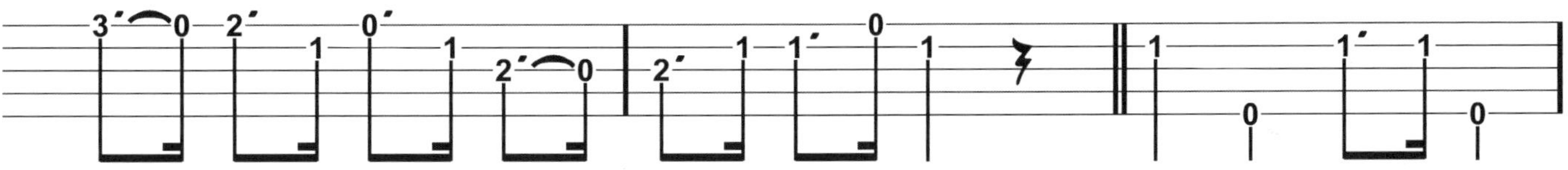

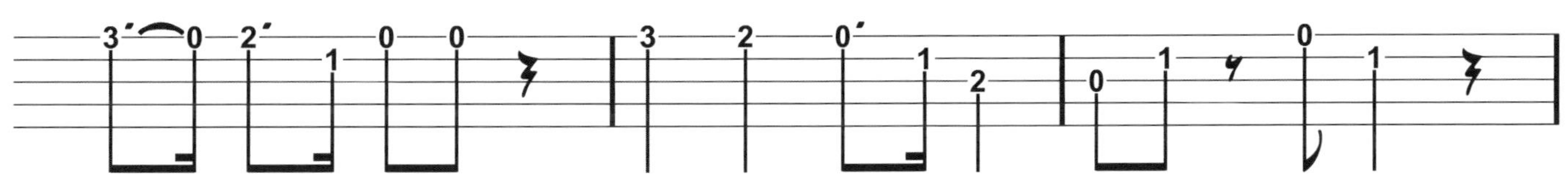

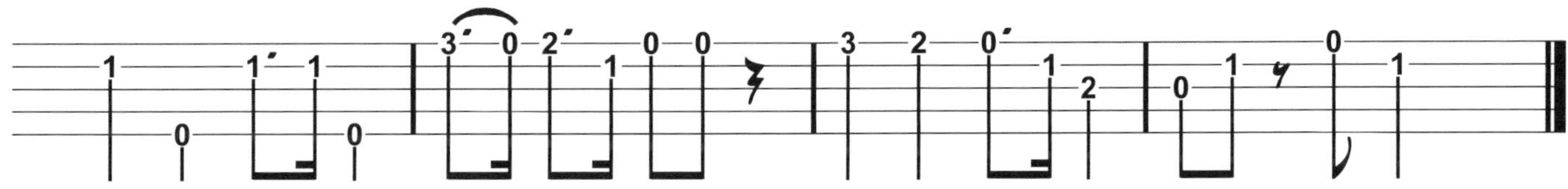

# Sand Jig I

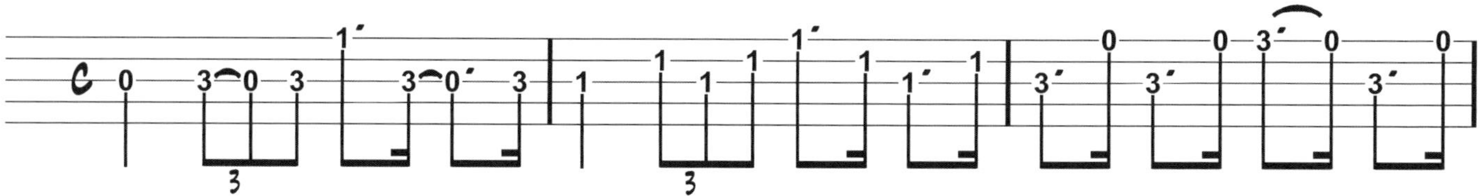
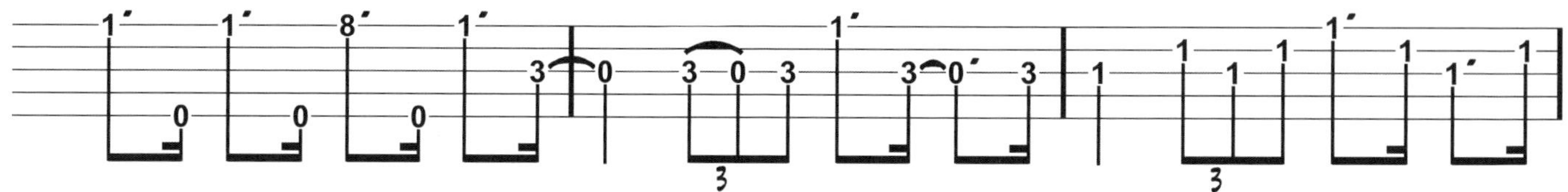
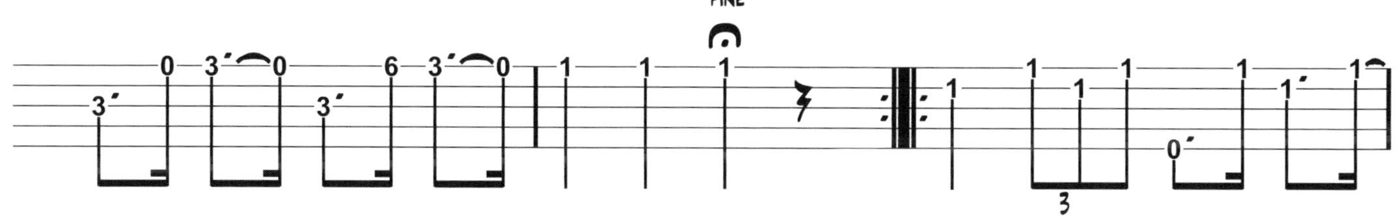

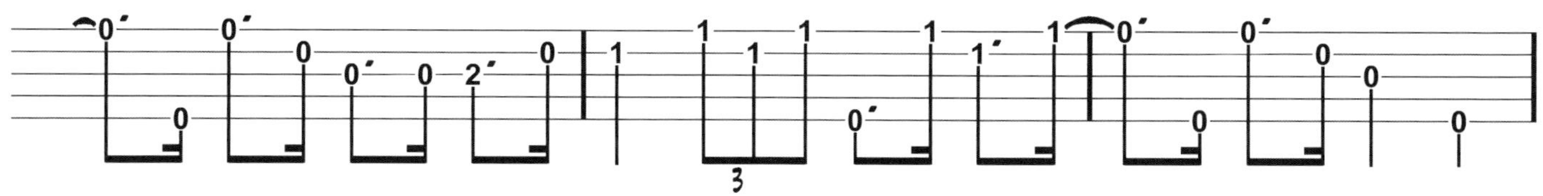
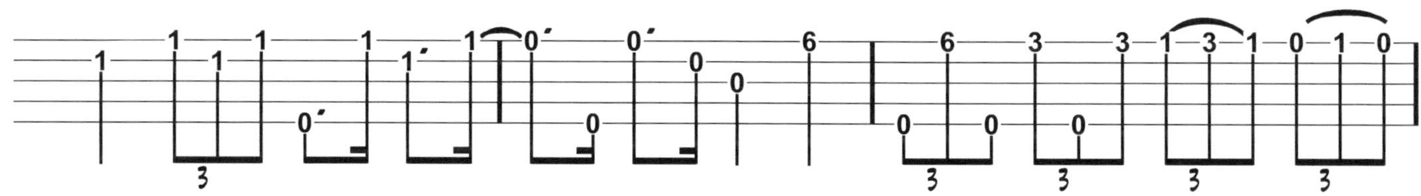
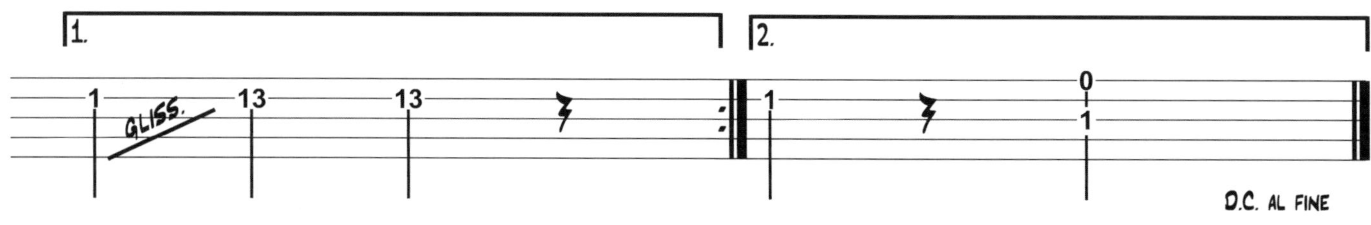

# Sand Jig II

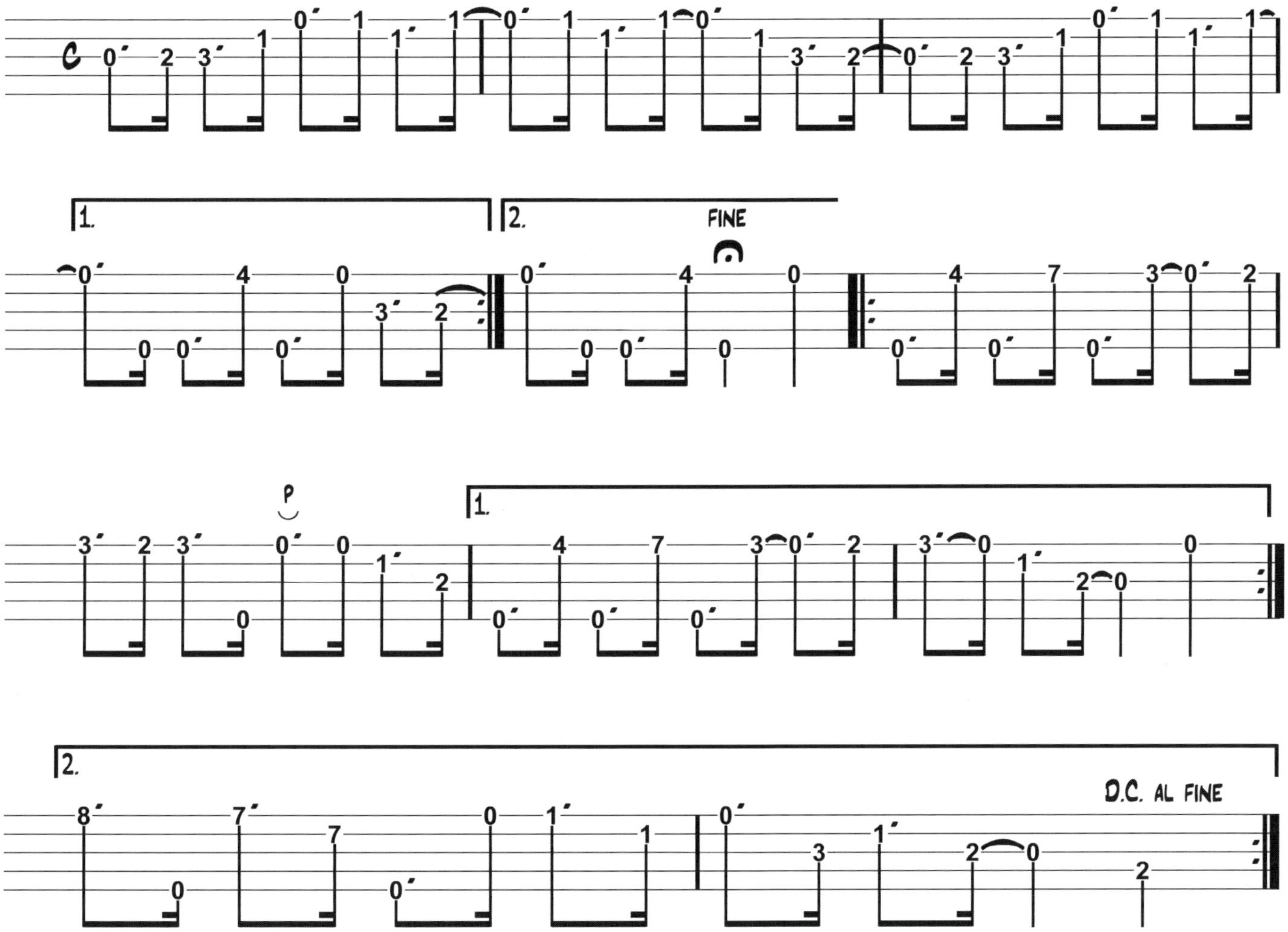

C

1. 2. FINE

P

1.

2. D.C. AL FINE

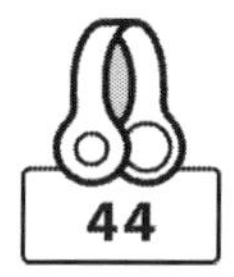


# Shins About the Fireside/Kate and Davy

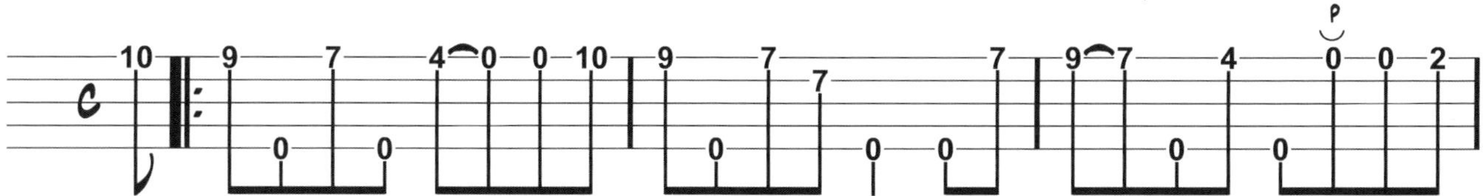

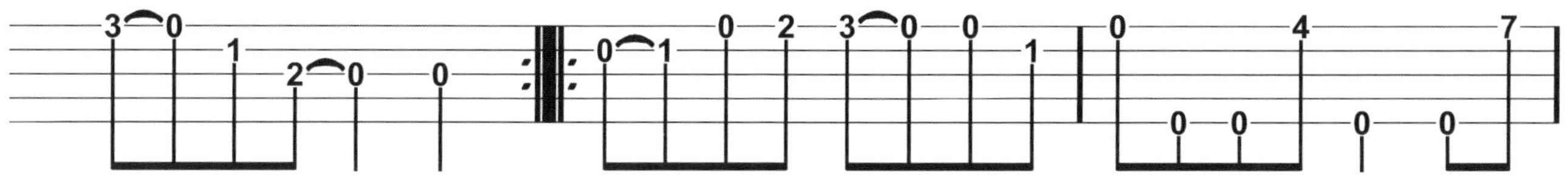

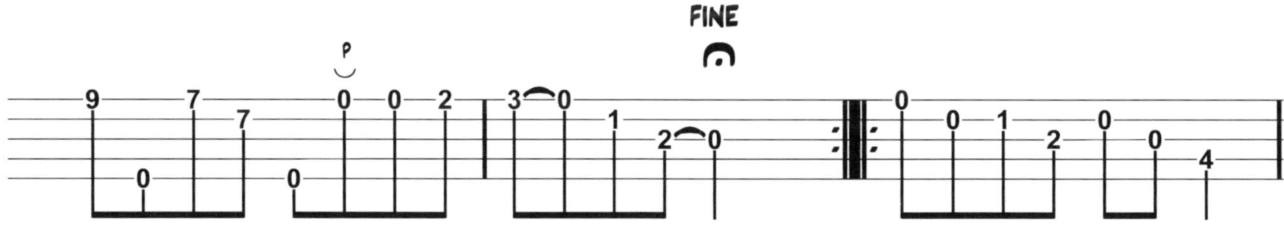


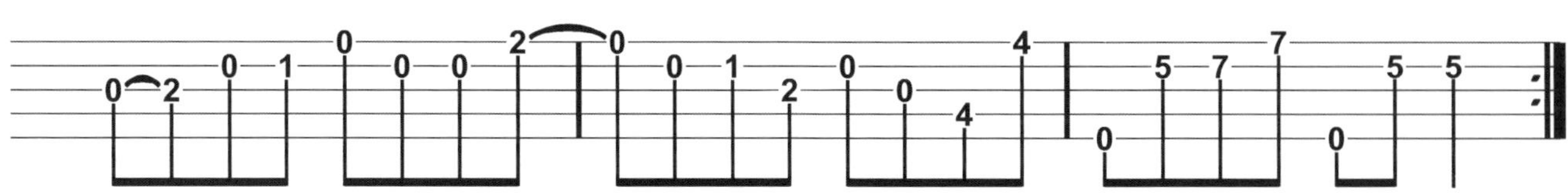

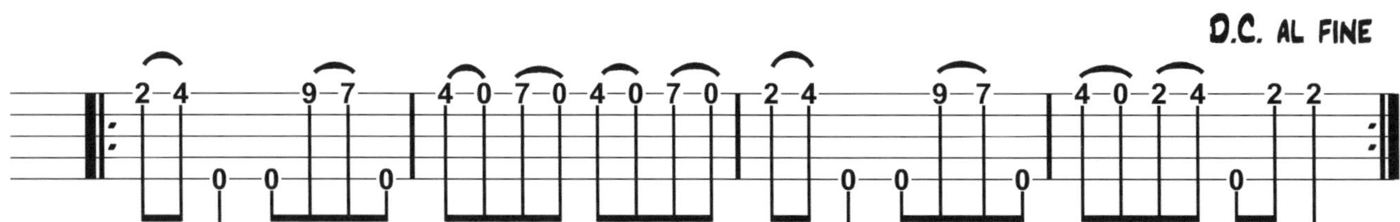

# The Black Brigade Camp Dance

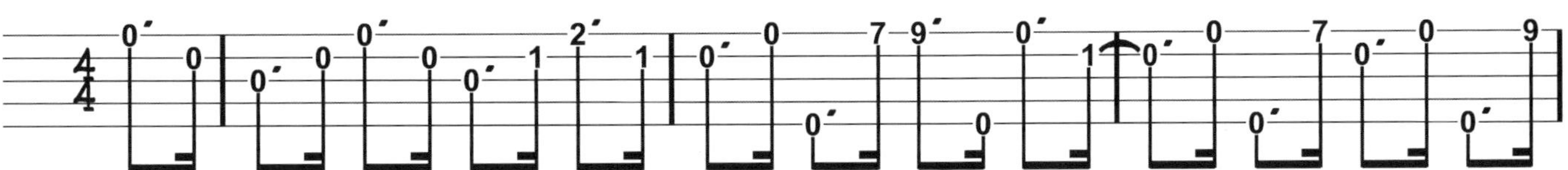

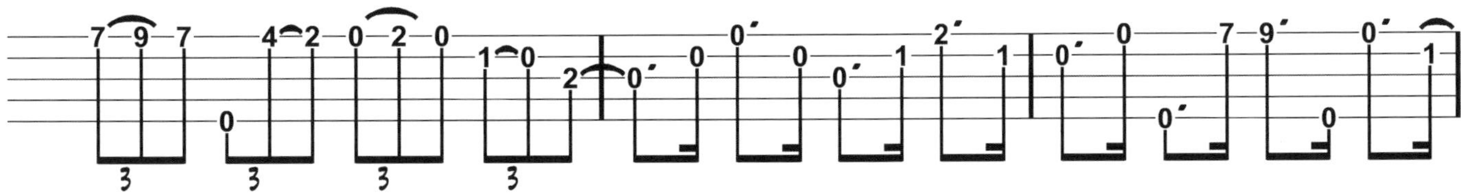

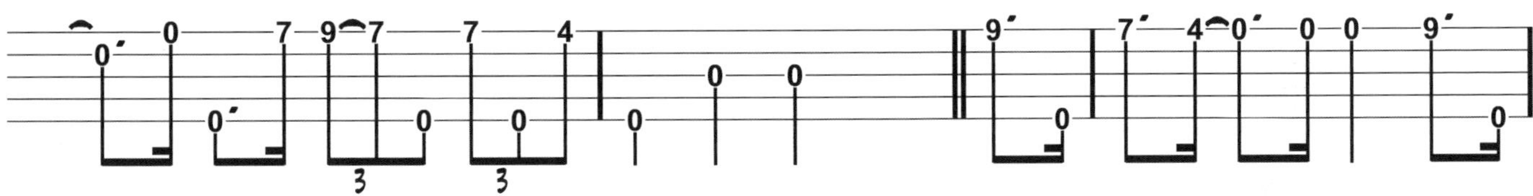

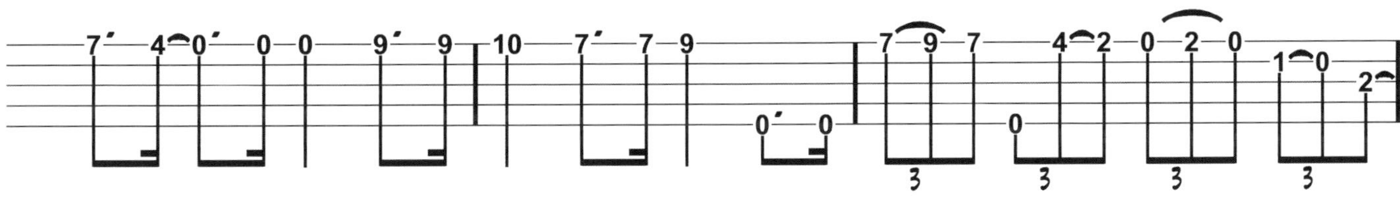

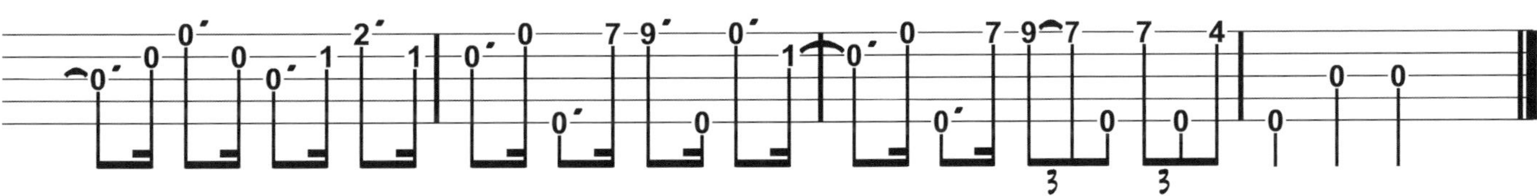

# Southern Rose

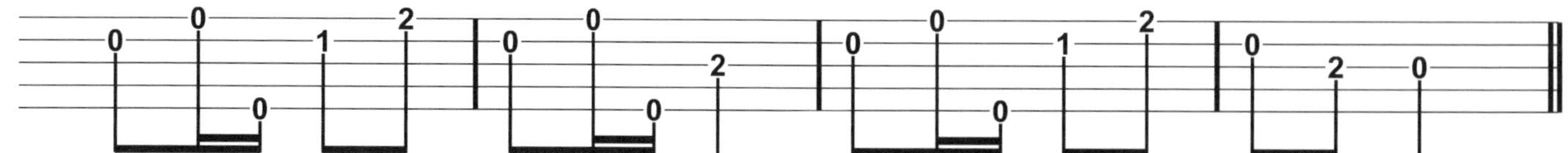

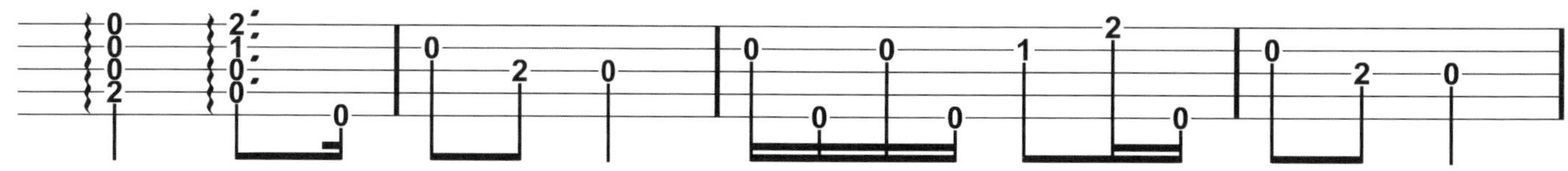

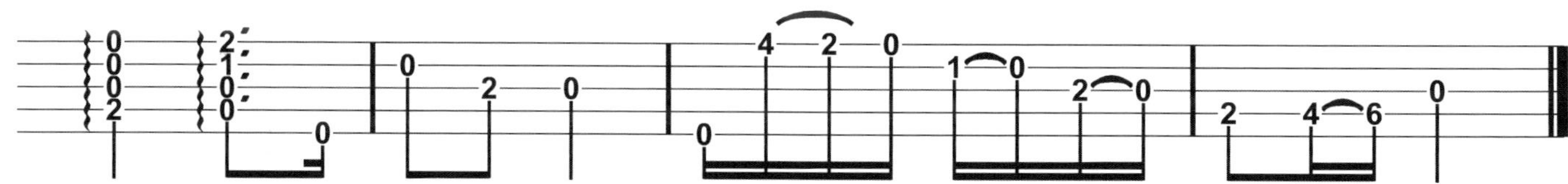

# The Keel-Row Reel

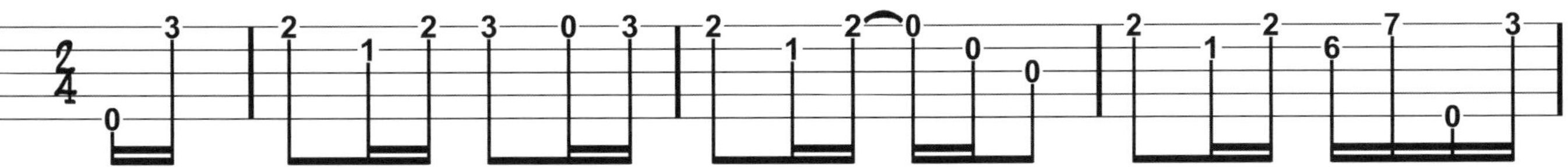

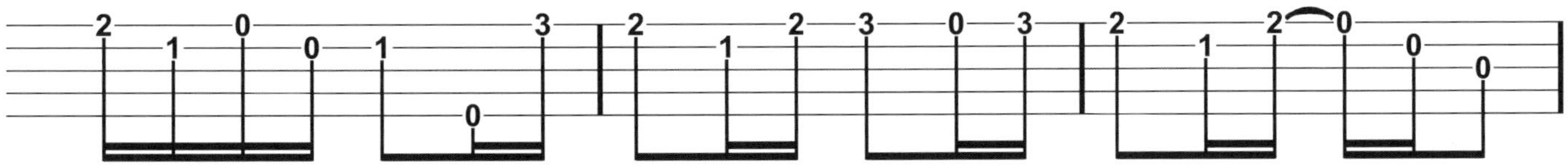

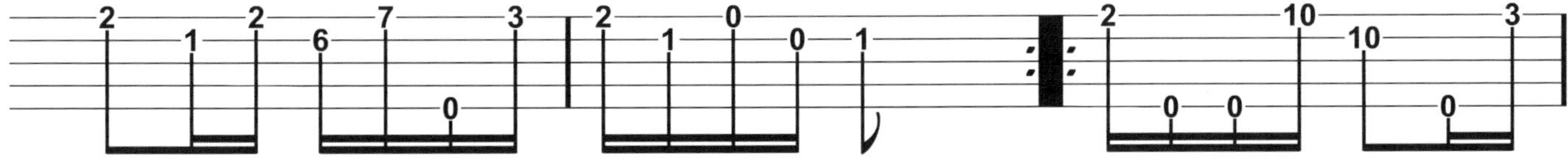

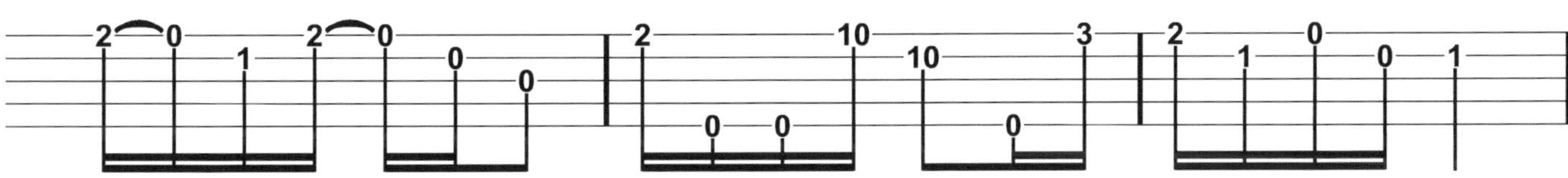

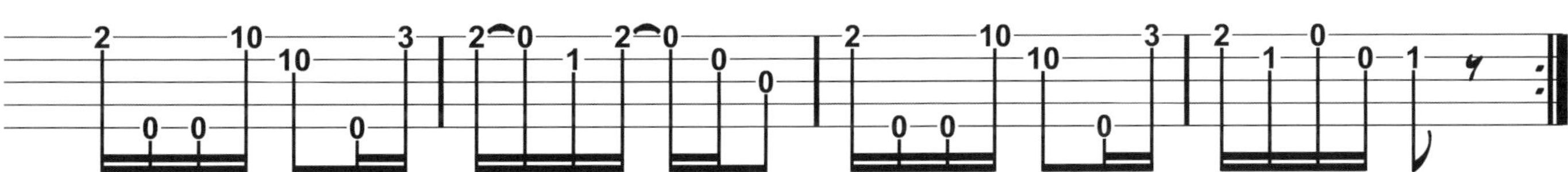

# Titania's Favorite Polka

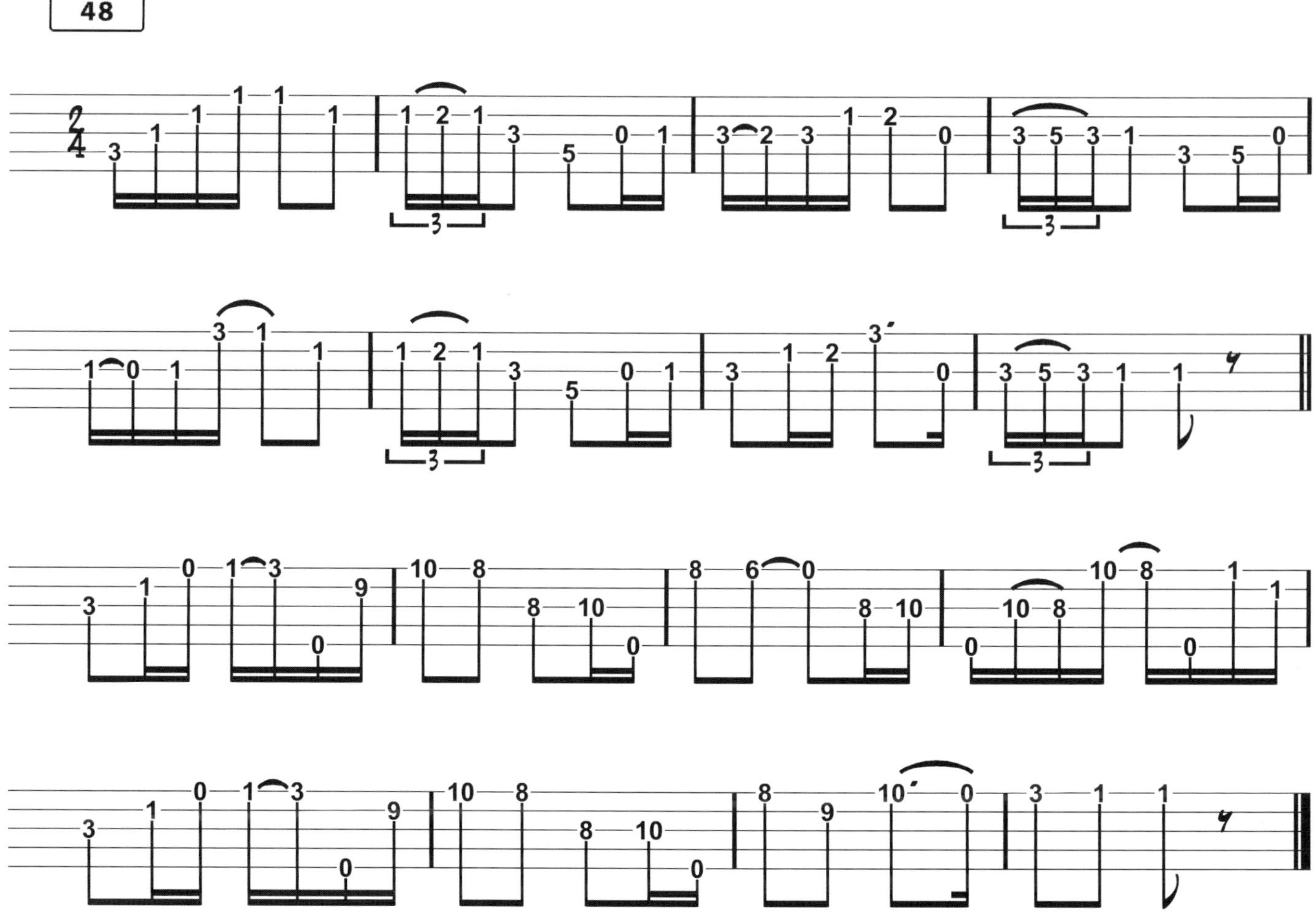

# Whiddon's Favorite Reel

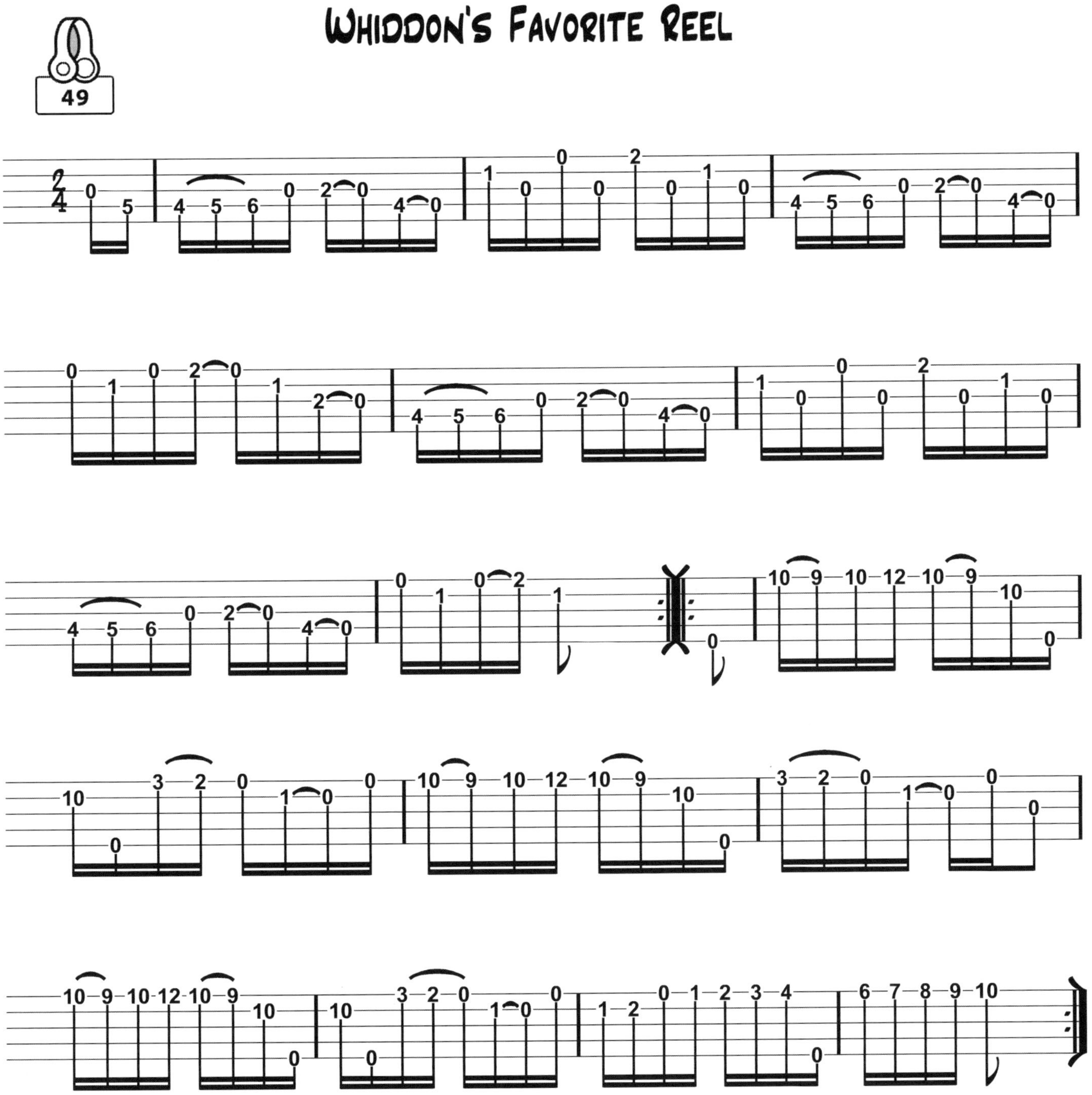

# Vivaldi's Concerto in D
## First Movement

50

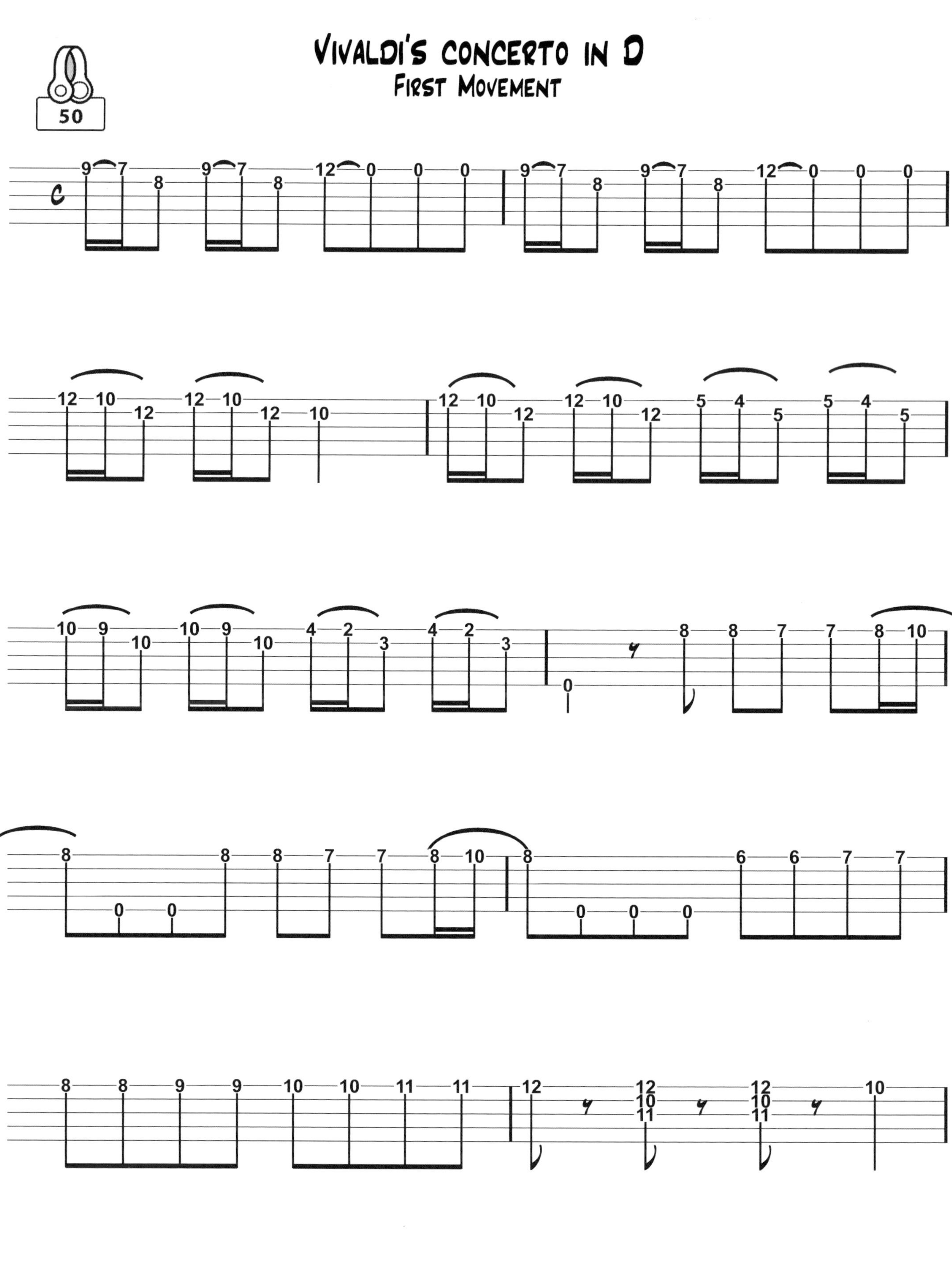

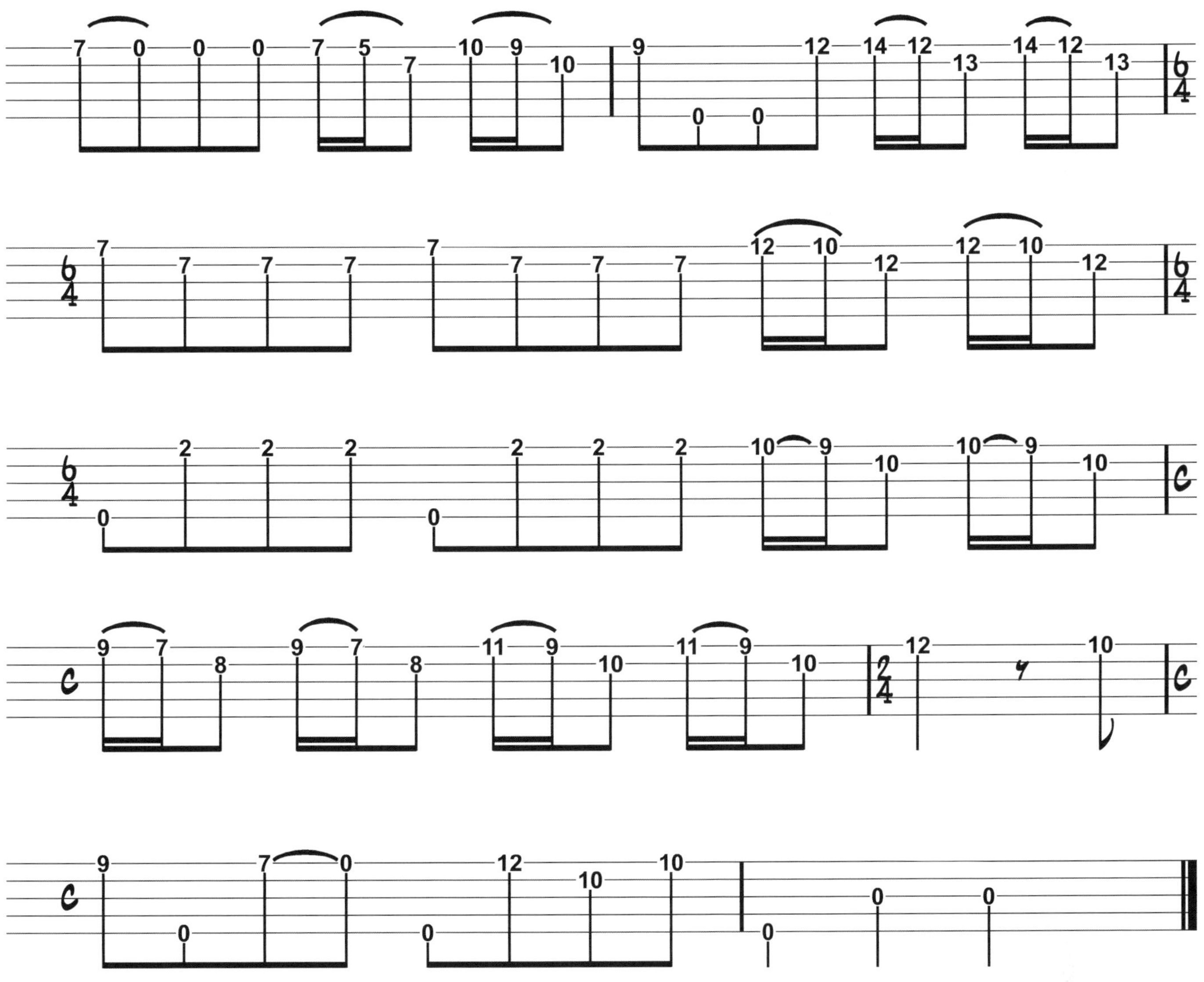

# Index



**Bold titles are the easiest to play.**